A Teacher's Guide
to the Information Highway

William Wresch
Department of Mathematics and Computing
University of Wisconsin-Stevens Point

Merrill,
an imprint of Prentice Hall
Upper Saddle River, New Jersey   *Columbus, Ohio*

Editor: Debra A. Stollenwerk
Production Editor: Alexandrina Benedicto Wolf
Design Coordinator: Karrie M. Converse
Cover Designer: Brian Deep
Cover photo: ©Charles O'Rear--Westlight
Production Manager: Laura Messerly
Director of Marketing: Kevin Flanagan
Advertising/Marketing Coordinator: Julie Shough

This book was set in Times Roman by Prentice Hall and was printed and bound by
Quebecor Printing/Book Press. The cover was printed by Phoenix Color Corp.

© 1997 by Prentice-Hall, Inc.
Simon & Schuster/A Viacom Company
Upper Saddle River, New Jersey 07458

Printed in the United States of America

10 9 8 7 6 5 4 3 2 1

ISBN: 0-13-621558-0

Prentice-Hall International (UK) Limited, *London*
Prentice-Hall of Australia Pty. Limited, *Sydney*
Prentice-Hall of Canada, Inc., *Toronto*
Prentice-Hall Hispanoamericana, S.A., *Mexico*
Prentice-Hall of India Private Limited, *New Delhi*
Prentice-Hall of Japan, Inc., *Tokyo*
Simon & Schuster Asia Pte. Ltd., *Singapore*
Editora Prentice-Hall do Brasil, Lrda., *Rio de Janeiro*

Preface

When we began work on *A Teacher's Guide to the Information Highway*, we had a very direct goal. Our university was being approached by classroom teachers who had an immediate need to know about the Internet. Their school was being wired up or was slated for wiring and teachers needed to know what implications this new thing--the Internet--would have on their teaching. Their question to us was almost always some version of this: "How can I us the Internet when I teach X?" They seldom asked about how the Internet worked, and rarely wanted to know about its history. They were busy teachers and wanted to know what other busy teachers were doing with this new resource.

So we set out to answer their question. With a grant from Ameritech and a television crew on loan from our university, we started visiting schools and videotaping classes. Many tapes and many interviews later, we had a 15-week course ready to air. First it went out to teachers in Wisconsin, and then the Public Broadcasting System (PBS) picked it up for distribution through their Adult Learning Satellite Service. We went national. Along the way I wrote this book as a way of telling some of the same stories and providing much of the background that there isn't time to cover in a 28 minute broadcast.

Those tapes and this book have the same orientation. First, we focus on curriculum. We see the Internet as an exciting way to teach the traditional subjects. To us, the Internet is not a new subject to be taught, but a road that brings new information to the old curriculum.

Second we decided the best way to show teachers how to use the Internet was to talk about the successful experience of teachers who were already using it. We visited classrooms in Milwaukee, Platteville, Stevens Point, and Rosholt, Wisconsin, and taped teachers and students as they moved through assignments. My television crew and I were very impressed by what we saw. We quickly decided that while I could provide some theoretical background, most of our efforts should consist of letting teachers talk for themselves. Other teachers would immediately see the value of their work and would follow suit.

What we decided not to do was get too caught up in the technology. However, we couldn't totally ignore it. For one thing some teachers find it interesting, and all teachers need to know at least the basics of telecommunications. But there are reasonable limits. The Internet is becoming easier to use all the time, and with the advent of the World Wide Web, information access requires far less technical expertise than it did just a few years back. Few teachers will ever use Telnet or ftp now that the Web is available. Few will need to know what a parity bit is. Rather than devoting chapter after chapter to information few teachers will ever use, we decided to focus on what teachers do need to know--how to teach with these new resources.

Structure of the Book

The objectives just discussed led directly to the structure of this book.

Getting Connected.   This section (Chapters 2-4) describes the basics of email, Gopher, and the World Wide Web. While there is some technical description of each, the real focus of each chapter is the classroom application of each resource. What might a teacher do with email, Gopher, or the World Wide Web? In each case we have answered that question by describing classroom practices of experienced teachers.

Curriculum Integration. These five chapters (Chapters 5-9) move from the general to the particular. First, what kinds of projects and cooperative activities seem to grow out of telecommunications? What general principles apply? What kinds of choices do you have? Then, how do you get students started? What do they need to know to be successful users of this technology.

Chapters 7-9 give detailed examples of projects in major curricular areas. From science and math to history and English, what resources are on-line and how can those resources best be used in the classroom?

Key Perspectives. While the classroom may be the focal point for curriculum integration, there are several other perspectives teachers need to have. First, what is happening in school libraries? These often have Internet connections and are making significant investments in on-line resources. Second, while teachers are rightly concerned first about their students, there are significant professional resources on-line for teachers as well. Knowing about these resources can help teachers advance professionally. Third, many decisions about technology will be made at the district level. As teachers join planning committees and implementation teams, they can benefit from the work of other districts that have already invested in the technology.

An then there is the larger world. We say one of the principal reasons to get on-line is to break out of the isolation of the typical classroom. But while linking to the rest of the world is exciting, it also brings teachers face to face with the practical limits their peers face in the developing world. How can we link to those other classes and make the most of that limited resource?

Hooking Up to the Internet. This section begins with a chapter on hardware. What links in the communications systems do teachers need to know about and what technical choices do they have? The next chapter turns to the first issue most teachers face--how do they get real access, not just an hour here and there. It describes state and national initiatives that are helping make telecommunications links more commonly available. And then there is the future. As we work to get on-line today, are there ways we can avoid investing in the Beta tapes of tomorrow? No guesses are perfect, but there are some trends that are emerging and can be used to guide planning.

Resources for Educators. This book and the tape series come with a Web site that has important educational links. The appendix describes those links. It should be a good starting place for workshops and inservices .

Features of this Book

You will find a number of features that make this book especially useful.

A Curriculum Focus. For each of the major curriculum areas there are specific examples of classroom uses. Science teachers describe connecting to professional scientists. English teachers describe writing projects. For each discipline, experienced teachers offer their suggestions.

Project Descriptions. Each chapter contains multiple examples of projects teachers have initiated on the Internet. They describe their objective, how they got started, and what resources they used. It should be easy for anyone using the Internet for the first time to follow these models.

Resource Lists. Teachers want to know what is on the Internet in their field. Major World Wide Web and email resources are listed in each chapter and again in the final chapter. The first time teachers use this book, they should find resources they will want to use in their classroom.

Supplements. Although this book can be used alone, there are two significant resources that are available.

- **World Wide Web Site.** A large Web site has been created for this book with links to more than 100 educational Web sites and supplemental materials. Located at **http://www.uwsp.edu/acad/math/infohwy.html** the site is constantly upgraded to ensure the latest resources are quickly available.

- **Video Programs.** A new series of video programs based on the book is also available via satellite from the PBS Adult Learning Satellite Service (ALS). Fifteen 30-minute programs guide teachers through the Internet. Filmed mainly in schools, the series focuses on practical classroom used from grades one to twelve. The program also highlights all the major World Wide Web sites of interest to teachers. Check with your Director of Continuing Education or Distance Education Coordinator for schedule information, or call PBS ALS at 1-800-257-2578.

Acknowledgments

A large number of people helped with this project. I am especially grateful to the teachers who invited us into their class and let us visit with their students. These individuals made this project possible.

William Andrekopoulus, Principal; John Thompson, Social Studies Teacher--Fritsche Middle School, Milwaukee, WI

Jan Baker, Librarian; Richard Upton, Science Teacher; William Grutz, Information Systems Manager; Loras Kruser, Principal; Phyllis J. Koeller, Media Specialist; Dean Isaacson, Superintendent--Platteville Public Schools, WI

Terri Iverson, Director of Media and Telecommunications--CESA #3, Platteville, WI

Jeffrey Tepp and Dan Gagnon, Math Teachers--Ben Franklin Junior High, Stevens Point, WI

Kathleen Martinson, District Administrator; Jim Grygleski, Social Studies Teacher; Phil Smith, Grade School Teacher; Gregory Kliss, Fourth Grade Teacher; Erwin Roth, Principal; Kenneth Camlek, Elementary Principal; Helen Adams, Media Specialist; Linda Trzebiatowski, Physical Education Instructor; Cindy Byers, Gifted and Talented Coordinator; Lorra Letko Walton, Spanish Teacher; Mike Roberts and Dave Eschenbach, Rosholt School Board; Susan Tupper, K-8 Media Specialist; Ann Parker, English Teacher, Rosholt High School--Rosholt, WI

In addition we were able to call on the professional expertise of these technology leaders: Gordon Hanson and Neah Lohr, Wisconsin Department of Public Instruction; Tom Taibl, Rich Maganini, Mike James, John Kolman, and Richard Perisho, Ameritech; Lee Alley, University of Wisconsin System Administrator; Neil Trilling, Center for Community Computing, University of Wisconsin-Milwaukee; and Arne Arneson and Pat Paul, Librarians, University of Wisconsin-Stevens Point.

I am also indebted to the following reviewers for their invaluable feedback: Janet L. Bohren, University of Cincinnati; Leticia Ekhaml, State University of West Georgia; Kim H. Foreman, San Francisco State University; Larry Hannah, California State University, Sacramento; Elizabeth T. Joseph, Slippery Rock University; and Nancy Knupfer, Kansas State University.

William Wresch
bwresch@fsmail.uwsp.edu
http://www.uwsp.edu/acad/math/infohwy.html

Brief Contents

Contents

HOOKING UP TO THE INTERNET

RESOURCES FOR EDUCATORS

Chapter 1
Introduction: What's Out There?

⌨ *"When are you most afraid?" (Question asked by a Seattle high school student via email to a friend in Tel Aviv during the Gulf War.)*

AN EXAMPLE

In 1989, Jeff Golub's Seattle, Washington high school students joined the Learning Network. A commercial venture that links school rooms around the world, his students were put in a group with twelve other schools--eight in the US and four in Europe. Assigned the task of exploring global pollution, Golub's class gathered data and once each class period one student would go to the computer in the back of the room, print off information received from the other schools, and type in the information gathered in Seattle.

The endeavor was very organized, very scholarly, very predictable. Students enjoyed having daily contact with their peers around the world, but the quality of the contacts didn't exactly compete with MTV. Then one day a student in West Berlin broke the rules and forgot to sent a message on local pollution. Instead, he wrote about what he had seen the night before. He had

1

been to the wall. So had lots of other people. He wasn't sure what was going on, but people were saying the wall might come down. End of message. Each morning for the next two weeks, students rushed early to their Seattle classroom to read what was happening at the wall. The pollution assignment was abandoned. Golub and other teachers tried to teach 16 year old Seattle students about the history and geography of Berlin, starting with pictures of "The Wall." Students balanced classroom lectures with personal messages and questions to their friend in Berlin. Finally after two weeks came the longest message of them all--"The wall is down. I saw my grandmother last night. She came through the wall."--screen after screen of eye witness description from a peer.

To the students in that Seattle classroom, history was no longer dry lectures and sanitized textbooks cleared by endless state committees. History was a young boy in Berlin writing about his grandmother.

Two years later Golub's class was again hooked to the Learning Network. A new crop of 16 year olds was linked to 11 classrooms--7 in the US, 3 in Europe, 1 in Tel Aviv. The research subject was pollution again and students collected local information and shared it with the other schools. The process was interesting, but routine. Then one day one of the girls in Tel Aviv started her message with "Last night the Scuds landed" and described her neighborhood. And once again, day after day, the students in Seattle ran into their classroom in the morning to check their email. What had happened? Were they OK? The Seattle students sent questions and messages of support. The Tel Aviv students described what their lives had become.

At one point one of the Seattle students asked, "When are you most afraid?" The answer from the teenagers in Tel Aviv? They were afraid to take showers. Wet, naked, soapy, they might not hear the sirens, and if they did, they worried they might not make it to the sealed room in time to protect them from any poisoned gas. The kids in Seattle had long talks, and lots of quiet moments, over that revelation.

Microcomputers have been in schools for well over a decade now. They have been used to record attendance, to drill multiplication tables, to process words, and to simulate taking a wagon train on the Oregon Trail. But nothing compares with the impact they have had now that teachers are using them to connect students to students. Now even young students can receive very personal information instantly from across the world.

OUR FOCUS

Jeff Golub's story is being repeated by teachers all over the globe. They suddenly have wholly new opportunities to connect their students to a world of information and people. With so many teachers doing so many interesting things, how can we even begin to look at all the possibilities? We will do just what you might do in your classroom--we will build our discussion around five main questions.

1. How do I link to these new information resources? It is one thing to know that there are millions of people and information sites at the other end of your computer's cable. It is another to know how to get to those places. We will focus on the two most significant approaches to information: email and the World Wide Web. Email is your link to people, while the Web is your link to "sites," places where information is stored and is publicly retrievable.

2. How might that information fit into existing curricula? One of our jobs as teachers is to make sense out of information--connect it into meaningful units for our students. Our challenges with these new sources are threefold.

First, there is much new information, and we will need time to find it and learn it ourselves, before telling our students about it. It is as if your school had just added a ten-story library. We need to know what is where.

Second, the information is changing rapidly. It is growing, it is moving, and some of it is disappearing. To stay with the library metaphor, our current situation would be akin to having a library that grew over night, everynight, and had all the shelves on rollers so you were never totally sure where you would find things in the morning.

Third, students can take a new relationship to this information. They can use email to speak directly to major historical figures (Rosa Parks holds conversation hours over America Online). They can set up their own Web pages and publish their writings. They can work jointly on projects with students in another state or another nation. This is all very interesting, but it means a new relationship between students and information--a relationship we will have to negotiate carefully.

So we will have some interesting opportunities and challenges as we take the wide expanse of the new information sites and merge them meaningfully into our core studies.

3. What challenges does the new technology present to teachers, students, libraries and school districts? There are thousands of teachers already using telecommunications with great success, so obviously all current challenges can be overcome, but it is always easier to overcome a problem if you already understand that problem and can learn from the experience of others. What are the challenges?

For teachers, the main need seems to be to keep up to date with all the resources coming on-line. Fortunately, there are a number of resources to make this a reasonable task.

For students, the problem is more subtle. It would seem all they would need to know is how to use one or two more computer programs, a skill they seem to acquire quite easily. But the challenge is more complex than that. The information they will find is information that hasn't been put through the filtering process that normally is performed by the school librarian and the district textbook committee.

Yes, they can hook to the world--*all* of the world. Some of that world is exciting, some of that world is crazy. Some of that world has value, some of that world is advertising and empty boasts. They need some help in telling the difference.

For libraries, the problem is finding a successful balance between the continuing need for print resources and the growing desire for digital resources. They also have to know how to pay for both at a time when few schools have extra money.

Districts need to plan for massive new wiring, new expenses, and how to deal with the few students who will decide the Internet is a great way to read the digital version of Playboy. Responding to such problems will require special technical and political abilities. It will also require the awareness and support of all the teachers in the district.

4. What hardware do we need? What hardware will we need in the future? It is a mistake to spend too much time with the details of computer links and phone systems. Yet teachers need to have some general understanding of how hardware works. They need to know what equipment to order and what systems should be installed in our schools.

5. What are the main electronic resources for teachers? By one calculation, five thousand Web pages are being added to the World Wide Web each day. It would seem impossible to keep track of all the ones that would be useful to teachers. Fortunately, you don't have to. There are kind souls who spend much of their day looking for good educational pages and adding references to them. Once you know the location of four or five main index pages, you can keep up with most of the major developments in telecommunications. We will describe these resources for you.

 DISCUSSION QUESTIONS

A Web site has been built for this course. The address is
> **http://www.uwsp.edu/acad/math/infohwy.html**

Figure 1-1 shows what the page looks like.
   Much of the Web site contains links to curricular materials. Visit the site and click on a site or two in your academic area.

1. How would you characterize the kind of information that is available on-line? What makes it different from the kind of information we could get in the past? How much are these differences *worth*?

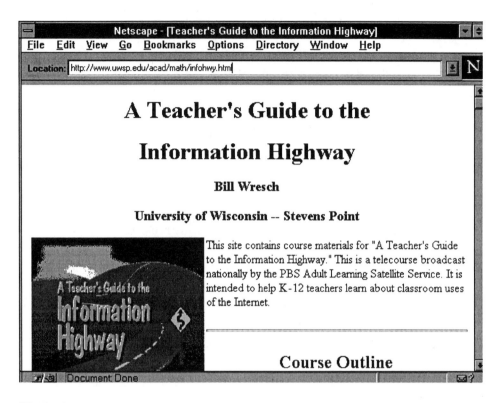

Figure 1-1

2. Find a page that covers materials you might like to show your students or use as part of a project. How might you integrate this information with current assignments? With current textbooks?

3. Parents are very concerned about students finding dangerous materials on the Net. How would you describe these curricular sites to a parent? Which one would you bring up for a quick PTO demonstration?

Chapter 2
Electronic Mail to the World

 ## OVERVIEW

Over twenty million people are connected to the Internet worldwide, with additional millions connected to other large networks. Schools are using this technology more and more to share information with schools in other parts of the world. This chapter describes some of the fundamentals of these linkages.

BACKGROUND

Networks

Computers can be connected in many ways. A Local Area Network (LAN) is a linkage of two to thirty computers, usually in the same room. Each computer is connected to a central computer, or *server*. The server acts as a switching station and storage location for all the other computers on the network. Each computer can send messages to the server--*upload*, or receive messages from the server--*download*. All traffic from one computer to another is routed through the server. It is the hub of all activity.

A Wide Area Network (WAN) links single computers or groups of computers to each other. WANs are more complicated than LANs in that there are usually greater distances involved for communication, greater numbers of machines, and often different kinds of machines. When one computer sends a message it first has to go to a local server, which has to know whether the message is intended for the local group of computers or whether it has to go off to a distant group. If it goes off to a distant group, the server has to do the routing of the message and may need to change the message so it is compatible with distant messaging systems.

Take, for example, a message one of your students, Susan, might send to another student, Marie, in a different middle school. As long as Susan is sending messages to other students in the local Macintosh lab (LAN), the message won't go far and will be picked up by a computer that is the same kind as hers, running the same software as hers. The minute the message needs to leave the building the process gets more complicated. The Macintosh server has to know that the message is intended for outside, and route it to an outside line. Since the machines on the receiving end may be IBM computers, the server may also have to "package" the message so that it can be understood when it gets there. This problem of routing and packaging for different computer systems is the principal work of larger networks.

The need to get messages across large distances and between very different computers is so great that a number of national and international networks have been established to handle the traffic. Some of these networks are private, like America Online or Prodigy. Others are public, like the Internet. Since the Internet is so large and so popular we should take a closer look at that network. But remember, the Internet is just one kind of larger network. It has competitors, all of which are trying to solve the same problem--how to get larger numbers of messages between different kinds of computers over great distances.

The Internet

The Internet is less a place than it is a process--an agreement to communicate information in a set way. It began with an effort at the US Defense Department to find some way to link military installations and university research centers so as to be able to handle large amounts of traffic under difficult circumstances. Enter Bob Taylor, director of computer research for the Department of Defense's Advanced Research Projects Agency. Taylor had already decided in 1966 that getting information from one computer to another might save money. But how? With one million dollars in expense money and the help of Larry Roberts of MIT, he built a small, four-computer network.

Taylor and Roberts made one decision early on that made all the difference. Information would be moved from one machine to another through packet switching, rather than circuit switching. The difference seems abstract, but turns out to be crucial. If I set up a circuit, like a phone connection from one point to another, data moves nicely once the circuit is set up, but setting up the circuit takes time, especially if the network grows to involve lots of computers in lots of places. A circuit is also vulnerable to disruption. Break the circuit at any point, and information flow stops. In times of peace, power outages or maintenance downtime break my circuit. In times of war, any event that destroys a switching node breaks my communication links.

What's the alternative? Make no complete circuit from a sending computer to a receiving computer. Instead, take any message, break it into chunks, or packets, and send them off. Each packet travels by whatever links are currently up and running, or currently have the smallest backlog. Packets arrive eventually by some route, are stored until the other packets arrive, and then are rejoined and presented to the receiving computer. Pieces of the original message may have taken five different routes to get to the receiver, but they get there eventually, and will get there even if much of the network has been disrupted.

The resulting communication network, the Internet, turns out to be pretty tough. It can handle days when computers go down, and it can handle days when traffic builds from more and more directions. We now have a way to get from here to there under some pretty rough circumstances. And millions of us are doing just that. As of this writing there are over twenty million people around the world using Internet.

So what is the Internet? At first it was an agreement over how data would be formatted for transfer from one computer to another. Now it is a collection of computers that agree they will use that format to send information back and forth. There is, however, an underlying structure to the Internet--a series of computers that do the main transfer and routing of messages. Those computers have owners and are connected by trunk lines that can carry heavy traffic. Originally the National Science Foundation covered the costs of key computers and data lines. Now we are moving to a hybrid system that will likely be partly supported by partly public money and partly commercial. The management and routing functions have to be paid for by someone. The debate over the National Information Infrastructure is partially a debate over who will pay for this underlying structure, and who will control it.

For the average teacher, the Internet is a gateway to twenty million computers--computers with information on them. Some of the computers link to professors, some to libraries, some to research centers. All the computers would be useful to get to. But remember there are two requirements in order to link. First, you need a wire to get you to the net. Second, you need to have your messages repackaged in the standard form of Internet messages. They have to be broken into the same packets as all the other messages streaming across the Internet. How do you make that connection? Usually you don't make the connection directly. You may need to link to a service provider. There are a growing number of companies that will serve as information brokers, taking your messages, reformatting them, and getting them onto the Internet. Needless to say, they require a fee for this service.

Email Addresses

In order to route messages to the proper destination, email needs an address just as much as a letter does. Each network has its own system for creating these addresses. Here are several examples:

Compuserve   76600.5567
Internet   bwresch@fsmail.uwsp.edu

Since Internet is the largest network, it is worth knowing a little bit about how addresses work. Essentially, you read an Internet address from right to left. The last section tells the country. If there is no country listed, the country is assumed to be the US. Here are countries you might encounter:

.uk   United Kingdom
.jp   Japan
.ca   Canada
.za   South Africa
.de   Germany

The next section of the address describes the type of site being addressed-- its domain. There are six basic domains:

com   company
edu   educational institution
gov   governmental body
mil   military
net   network gateway
org   private organization

The next section is the name of the institution itself. This is often followed by a subdivision marker--the name of a department or branch. Finally there is the @ sign and the name of the individual computer.

Do you get to make up your own address? No. All addresses have to be approved by the controlling authority of the Internet. If they weren't, two groups might pick the same address. For instance, does **vt.edu** refer to the University of Vermont, or Virginia Tech? Only one can have the address (it was claimed by Virginia Tech). Once the address has been approved, routing computers on the Internet know how to direct messages they encounter.

Sending Mail Between Major Networks

If you know a person's email address, your computer messaging system will handle much of the communication process. We will look at the details of the process in Chapter 13 when we follow a message through the computer and its modem. For the moment, though, it is necessary to consider one additional wrinkle. It is often the case that the teacher or student you wish to reach is on another network. You are hooked to Internet, they are hooked to America Online. Fortunately, there are gateways that link the largest networks. You signal your need to send a message to a different network, usually by attaching the name of that network to the address.

For example, if you are using Internet and wish to send a message to someone who uses the Compuserve network, you might take their usual address, 76609.4432, and add Compuserve to it. The result would be something like this:

76609.4432@compuserve.com

Your network will understand that the message needs to be routed to Compuserve, and it will direct your message to the right *gateway*. Once at the gateway, the bridging computer will do any repackaging of your message that may be needed for the other network.

Creating Electronic Mail Messages

There are a large number of electronic mail programs available. Each performs the same basic functions. They have a word processor to create the actual message, and boxes to collect the address and subject fields. Here is the email program I use (Figure 2-1). It uses the Windows operating system, so I just move a mouse from box to box and fill in the needed contents.

The place I need to exercise the most care is the address. Each letter has to be exactly right. There can be no extra spaces or punctuation. I also need to put periods between each of the address fields. If I make a mistake, the message will either go to the wrong place, or will be returned to me as undeliverable.

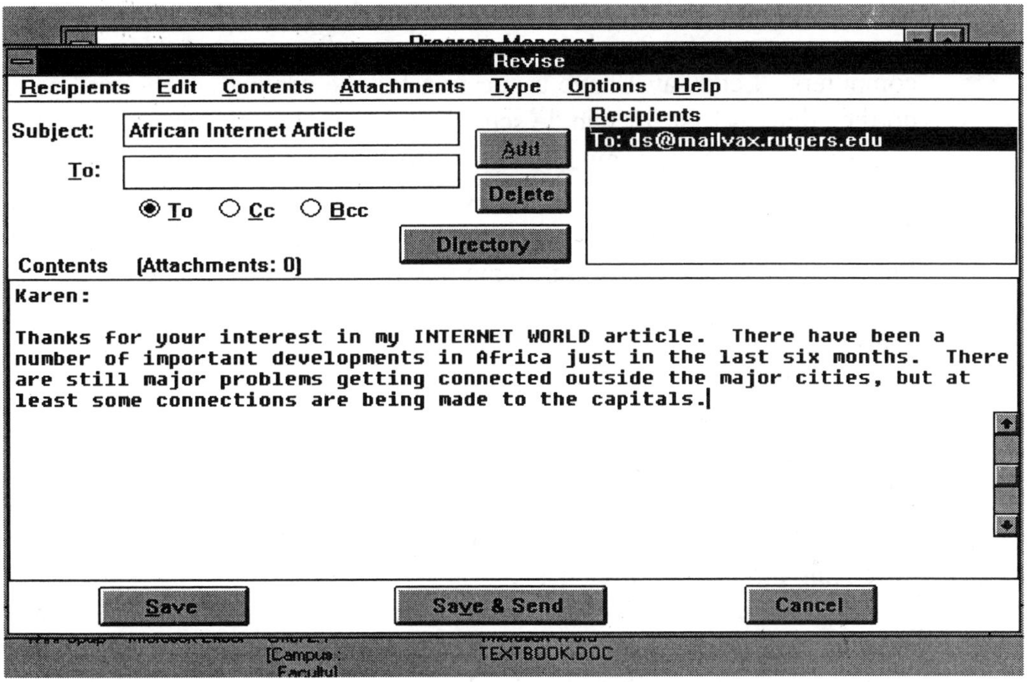

Figure 2-1

Electronic Mail Discussion Groups

While we think of paper mail as a message for a single person, electronic mail can just as easily be addressed to dozens or even hundreds of people simultaneously. This is the process used for discussion groups. At this point there are tens of thousands of electronic discussion groups in existence. Some are sponsored by professional organizations (most teacher's groups have set up discussion groups), others are created by interested individuals. We will look at how messaging systems work first, and then describe some of the more popular discussion groups.

Let's begin with an example. The Assembly for Computers in English (ACE) is a part of the National Council of Teachers of English. ACE has a discussion group for teachers who want to talk about teaching English with computers. Let's say I have a question for the group--which word processor do they think is best for middle school students? I send a message to the ACE computer. The ACE computer now stores my message. It then makes a copy of my message and sends a copy to each of the people in the discussion group. That could be five people or five hundred people. Each will see my question. Let's say most don't have an opinion about my question, but three do. They each write a response and send it to the ACE computer. The ACE computer stores their original answer and sends a copy to every person in the group. Each member of the group will see both my question and all the answers.

Because we can send messages to so many people simultaneously, such groups are a great source of information. With one letter you can get back fifty or one hundred answers. And, since everyone in the group can read the answers you got, they can also comment on the answers, clarifying points or describing different approaches.

On the downside, a large group can often generate so much mail that members are overwhelmed. If a group has one hundred members (and many are much larger), each member needs do only a little writing and the system is quickly overwhelmed. If each person makes just two comments a day, that is two hundred messages that will be sent to each member of the group. How many days a week do you have time to sit down to two hundred letters?

To try to control such volumes of mail, lists often employ a *moderator*. The function of this person is to keep trivial messages off the net, and to try to focus discussion around significant topics. Without a moderator, the volume of messages too frequently becomes a cacophony of unrelated questions and comments. Because the moderator needs to keep some messages off the net, there is an element of censorship involved, a prospect that bothers some users. Yet without some limits, lists often degenerate into a massive surplus of irrelevant messages.

Lists will generally state whether they are moderated or unmoderated, so potential members know what they are getting into.

In Chapter 10 we will look more closely at discussion lists for teachers.

PROJECT SUGGESTIONS

🖰   Modie Moore, a high school teacher in Connecticut, uses the America Online network to link to the Electronic Schoolhouse service. In his first on-line project, he and his class joined "Scrapbook USA" which linked his school to twenty others across the country. His students used that link to exchange research information with the other schools. Students explored subjects of their own choosing, sending early drafts over the network for comments from other students around the country.

🖰   In a second net project for his class, a teacher in Hawaii agreed to create an environmental newsletter on the network, with students in schools around the country sending in essays and research reports. Moore and his students read the other writings that had been posted, did some research on their own, and contributed their own research to the newsletter.

🖰   Moore started a third project called "Book Chat," in which his students described books they had written and made recommendations to other students about the books. They posted all their reactions on the Net, and then answered questions or had further discussions with other students who had also read and enjoyed the books.

Each of these projects connect students to other students, involve the sharing of written work, and give students an opportunity to "publish" their writing. Each would make a good project for you and your students.

DISCUSSION QUESTIONS

St. Olaf's College in St. Paul, Minnesota has an on-line clearinghouse of email addresses that is helpful for finding schools and students around the world. The address is:

http://www.stolaf.edu/network/iecc/

Here is its Web page:

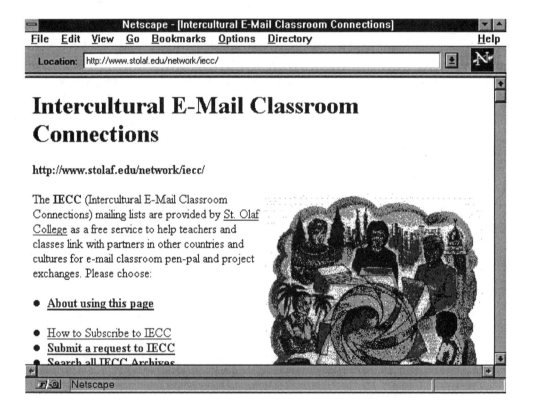

Click on the "Search IECC Archives" hyperlink to read about some of the schools that are interested in making connections.

1. Where do most schools seem to be?

2. What are most schools looking for?

3. If you can find a project that connects to something you teach, send an email message to the teacher and ask about the project. How is it going? Did they find many schools to share information with? What was the reaction of their students? What are students learning?

4. Teachers often have all their students write their message on word processors in a computer lab first. Then they check the messages and help students send the messages one at a time. Can you think of other ways to do quality control and resource management?

5. You sometimes hear that people are disappointed with email use in schools, calling it a fringe. They complain that the content of messages is little more than chitchat. If that is a problem, how do we ensure that real learning occurs as part of the email experience?

RECOMMENDED READINGS

Hafner, K. The Creators. *Wired*, December 1994, 152-154.

Moore, M. Beyond the Classroom Walls: AOL in the schools. *The ACE Newsletter*, Vol. IX, Winter-Spring 1995 (c/o Robert Royar, Department of English, Morehead State University, Morehead, KY 40351-1689)

Chapter 3
Getting Connected: Gopher

 ## OVERVIEW

What data are out there for students who wish to do research? One large collection of data is in Gopher servers. By maneuvering through the Gopher system, students can locate and retrieve materials to help with projects they are doing.

BACKGROUND

Universities and research centers often have large collections of reference material that they are willing to share. They put the material in digital form and leave it on computers that can be accessed through the Internet and other networks. These files of material can then be transferred over the Net. Whole books can be transferred in this way, as can photographs, research reports, or anything else that can be put in a digital form.

While vast amounts of information are now available, you can get the information only if you know where it is. Essentially, you need a card catalog for all the thousands of computers on the Internet. Creating such a catalog is no easy process because of all the thousands of sites involved and because the information available changes every day. You also need to know the commands to instruct one computer to copy information from another. These commands aren't all that complicated, but they are cumbersome and easy to mistype. The result is that lots of information is available, but getting to it (and getting it to you) can be more difficult than one would like. Several responses have been made to this problem. The two that are the best known are Gopher and the World Wide Web. We will look at Gopher in this chapter and the World Wide Web in the next.

Gopher History

Gopher was written in 1991 at the University of Minnesota (the gopher state). This software had three goals: Make it easy to find information, make it easy to get information, and make it easy to share information with others. It was originally written for use by students at the University of Minnesota, but the program was so effective and easy to use that other universities began adopting it as well. In the past several years it has become one of the standard access routes to information on the Internet. It is gradually being supplanted by the World Wide Web, but is still a significant information source, especially for simple texts.

The Gopher interface consists of a series of menus. It is also hierarchical. In other words, you start at the top level, and work your way down to specific information. For instance, if you wanted to find out what information was located in the library at UW-Platteville, you would start at the US, then Wisconsin, then Platteville, etc.

Here is a typical main menu (Figure 3-1). It lists local resources and provides access points to other gopher servers. It operates like any menu system. You move your mouse to the option you want, and press the button.

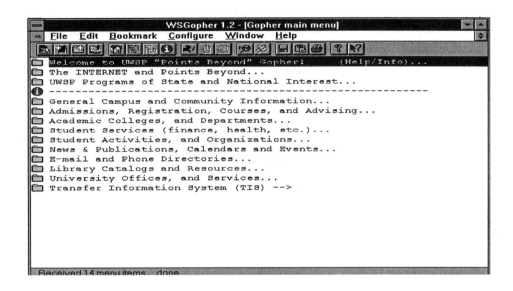

Figure 3-1

If we select **Internet and Points Beyond**... , we will get the following screen:

Let's assume we want to get information about Harvard University. Since the Gopher system is hierarchical, we would start with the US, then work our way down through the states until we got to Harvard. So we would select **USA Gopher servers**, then **Massachusetts**, then **Harvard**, and the screen would look something like this:

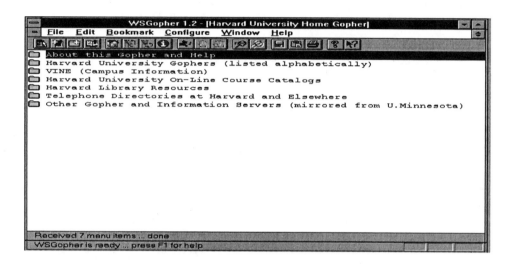

With just three clicks of our mouse, we have now accessed the main Gopher computer at Harvard, and can now see what resources are available there. Universities vary widely in the amount of information they will make available. Some make a substantial effort to put as much information out there as they can, others seem less interested. The choice is theirs. What Gopher does is make it easy for us to get to their site to see what they have made available.

Downloading Information

Once we have found something interesting, we will want to have the computer make a copy of it and move it from the computer at Harvard to our computer.

Once we have a copy, we can put it into a word processing document or other program of our own and do with it as we will (subject to copyright laws).

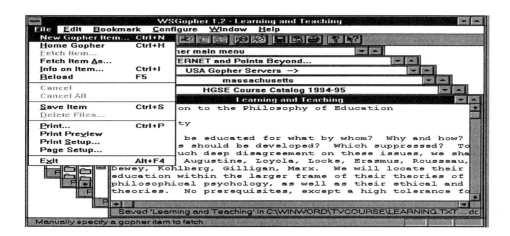

If I am running Gopher within a Windows environment, I just select **FILE** and look down the list of options for **Save Item**. If I choose to save the item I have picked, the current item on the screen (in this case a course description from the Harvard Graduate School of Education) will be copied to my computer and saved on a disk in my machine. I could then move that description to any word processor file and include it , for example, as a part of a paper I might be writing on available college courses on educational theory. In a matter of a few seconds, I have had my computer search a computer one thousand miles away, pick out something of interest to me, and bring back a copy for my use.

What's Available?

The short answer is, whatever organizations want to make available. They don't get paid for what they share, so they either have to have an education mission (like the Smithsonian), be altruistic, want publicity, or want to save mailing costs (or all four). In general, you see what organizations want you to see. For example, colleges will list their course catalogs, but probably won't list how much crime occurs on campus, or have counts of the number of professors being sued for sexual harassment. You need to be a wise information consumer.

Nevertheless, there are some valuable sources of information for both you and your students. For example, you will want to get to these gopher sites:

California
- San Francisco Unified Schools: links to lots of education gophers
- WELL: links to lots of education gophers

Michigan
- Environmental Education Gopher: project ideas and articles

Texas
- Texas Educational Network: links to other schools and teachers

Washington, DC
- The American Meteorological Society: weather forecasts and maps
- C-SPAN: classroom info, House of Representative votes
- Smithsonian Institution: pictures of volcanoes

Wisconsin
- Wisconsin State Agencies: current legislation, searchable by key word

Gopher in the Classroom

One of the most immediate demonstrations of how quickly information technology is changing is the overnight rise and fall of the Gopher system. Everyone's darling in 1990, by 1996 it was hard to find anyone talking about it. This is especially true in educational circles where the World Wide Web has exploded on the scene. Why the change? As you could see from the sample screen above, the gopher shows us words, words, words. It also has a hierarchical interface--much less fun than the hyperlinks of the Web.

It might be tempting, in view of the way the technological winds are blowing, to just ignore Gopher entirely. But there are three reasons why you may want to both teach your students about it and use it yourself.

1. Gopher servers still hold a great deal of information. In March of 1994 Gopher was used to transfer 700 gigabytes of information each month. (That is 700 billion characters of information, or about 700 million document pages). In 1994 it was used just as often as the World Wide Web. Its use has fallen off in the years since and the Web's use has grown, but it is still a formidable data repository. There are still quite a few documents out there that can be of use to you and your students. Any of the Gopher sites listed above will help you see just how much is there.

2. Gopher is less commercialized than the Web. If you catch any TV, you will spot Web addresses being touted by Ford, Coke, and the NBA. These are all attractive and have their uses, but the uses are not always principally educational. Gopher documents may be much more staid than their Web counterparts but that may be exactly what makes them attractive to teachers (if not to students).

3. Gopher navigation may be easier for some people. The very hierarchical orientation of the Gopher, where users move up and down obvious chains of locations, may make it easier to students to understand where they are. They are in the US, then California, then San Francisco, etc. They can make a mental map of where they are in cyberspace.

For all these reasons Gopher is living on, especially in university circles. It will continue to be an information resource for at least the next several years.

PROJECT SUGGESTIONS

⌐Ϙ   Cordelia Kohrman of Sheperd High School in Sheperd, Michigan uses Gopher for a research project about colleges.   She has each student do research on three colleges. They sift through campus information each college has put on-line, searching for colleges that have the most interesting programs, and learning about costs and living conditions. After they have gathered the information they need for their papers, she has a fun day in which students try to search for unique colleges--those with the smallest or largest ratio of girls to boys, the oddest extra-curricular activities, the most foreign students. Their findings are put in the form of charts and displayed on classroom bulletin boards.

⌐ **DISCUSSION QUESTIONS**

1. Information has to come from someplace. After you have looked through a number of Gopher sites, see if you can tell who the principal providers of Gopher information are. Do you have any theories for why some organizations place information on Gopher servers and others don't?

2. Once your students have some familiarity with the World Wide Web, you might have them compare Web sites and Gopher sites for the same organization, such as a university. Besides obvious differences in appearance, can they find other differences?

3. If the Gopher system does in fact disappear within the next few years as predicted, does that have a message for our students about what kind of information resources will predominate?

4. Look at the information resources published by the legislature of your state. Are they on Gopher? The Web? Both? Neither? What decisions are other states making about the provision of public information?

Chapter 4
Getting Connected:
The World Wide Web

 OVERVIEW

The World Wide Web is the newest form of data on the Internet, and certainly the most talked about. It combines an attractive interface with ease of use to establish itself as a monumental publishing opportunity. With five thousand new sites being created per day, a wealth of education materials are becoming available over this system.

BACKGROUND

In 1989 Tim Berners-Lee was working at CERN, the European Particle Physics Institute in Geneva. Researchers at several locations were preparing reports on joint research. Combining the documents they were preparing was often cumbersome and time consuming. Berners-Lee wanted a way to let these research groups write independently, but then later combine their work into a single document. He decided to create a hypertext system in which documents could be linked in many ways. Reading the resulting documents would be novel in that readers could jump from a topic in one document directly into a similar topic in a related document. At least they could if there were software to create this link.

To accomplish this end, Berners-Lee had to establish a language for creating hypertext, a systematic approach to moving such documents from one computer to another over networks, and a system of addresses. This took three years and a great deal of help gathered from electronic mail discussion groups, alt.hypertext and comp.infosystems.www (Wiggins, 36). At roughly the same time Marc Andreesen, a student at the University of Illinois, created Mosaic, a "browser," or interface to the system. Mosaic was attractive, relatively bug-free, and instantly popular. Meanwhile, important extensions were added so that the Web could handle images.

To those who were used to staring at screens of straight text, the Web looked like a totally different animal. It had color, multiple text sizes, and full color images. The old Internet was dull; the Web was beautiful. Suddenly it was cool to have a "home page" on the Web. Music groups, sports organizations, even the White House created home pages on the Web with attractive graphics and links to a variety of documents. You could download the President's latest press release or last year's draft picks just by clicking on a place on the screen.

NAVIGATING THE WORLD WIDE WEB

The Web is designed to give you several ways of moving from one "page" to another. Each page is a collection of information created by an individual or group and made available for your use.

1. Hypertext links. Any text on the screen that is underlined is a link to another "page." It is like a menu option. Just click on it with your mouse and you will jump to that location. On the following example (Figure 4-1)

- Search our Web
- What's New
- Internet and Points Beyond

are all hypertext links. Just click on those words and you will either search the local web, see what's new, or jump to the Internet.

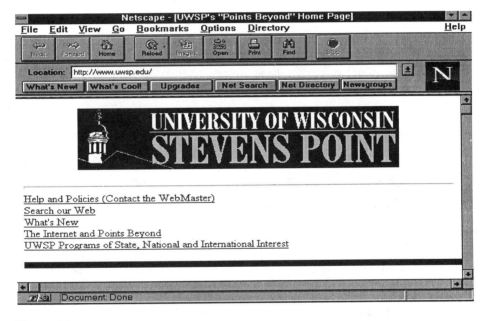

Figure 4-1

2. Buttons. Near the top of the screen are squares with "Back," "Forward," and "Home" in them. If you click on them you will go back to the last page you were on, forward to the next page in your sequence, or home to the first page on your screen when you started. Think of "Home" as your panic button. If you get too confused about where you are, just click there and you go back to where you began (click your heels and you are back in Kansas).

3. URLs. Every page has a Uniform Resource Locator, or address. If you know what that address is, you type it into the line that says "Location". The main URL for our campus is "**www.uwsp.edu**". You will find that on the screen whenever you start using the Web.

To enter a new address, move the mouse to the location line, and click. A vertical line should appear. This is the cursor and means the program is ready for you to begin. Erase the old address (but keep the initial **http://**), and type in the address you want. What are good addresses? There are many listed in the back of this book and on the course Web site (**http://www.uwsp.edu/acad/math/infohwy.html**), but here are a few that you might want to type in on your own to get a flavor for the range of information available over the Web:

http://www.cnn.com	*The CNN network*
www.zamnet.zm	*The home page for Zambia*
www.prenhall.com	*Listings for Prentice-Hall*
www.epic.org	*Electronic Privacy discussions*
www.sec.gov	*Securities & Exchange Commission*
thomas.loc.gov	*US Congress*
www.cbs.com	*The CBS network*
www.disney.com	*Disney*
gsn.org/gsn/gsn.projects.html	*Global Schoolroom Network*
www.unicc.org	*United Nations*

4. Search Engines. You can also move around the World Wide Web by using any of the search programs that are available. Yahoo is a good search program, as are Web Crawler and Alta Vista. To get to these search programs you type in their address as you would any other Web page.

Yahoo
http://www.yahoo.com

Yahoo will search for individual topics, but it also has lists of topics. These general headings can be a convenient starting place for someone who is searching for general information but isn't too sure where to go. Among its headings are Education and Internet, two popular areas for student research.

Webcrawler
http://query.webcrawler.com

Webcrawler performs searches in a manner similar to Yahoo. It has a good topics list that can be useful for initial browsing.

Alta Vista
http://www.altavista.digital.com

Alta Vista is the current darling of search programs because it searches not only titles of Web pages, but their entire contents (and does so in seconds). If you were searching for a person, say Mark Twain, it would find not only all the sites that specialize in him (quite a few do), but it would also find all sites that even mentioned him in passing.

How does a search work? We might use Yahoo as an example and do a search for a common topic, NASA. We would begin by typing the search word in the appropriate area of the screen, and then click on "Search." Figure 4-2 shows what the screen would look like.

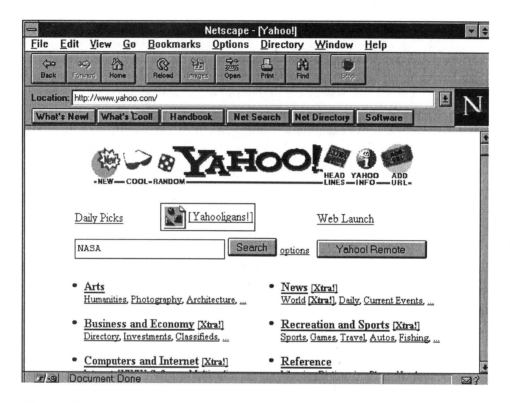

Figure 4-2

Yahoo would then look for all sites that have "NASA" in their name. Figure 4-3 shows the result of that search.

Yahoo was able to find 362 Web sites that contained NASA in their description. It will display each of them if requested. Once you have seen a description that looks like the site you want, you just click on the underlined portion of the screen, and Yahoo will take you directly to that Web site.

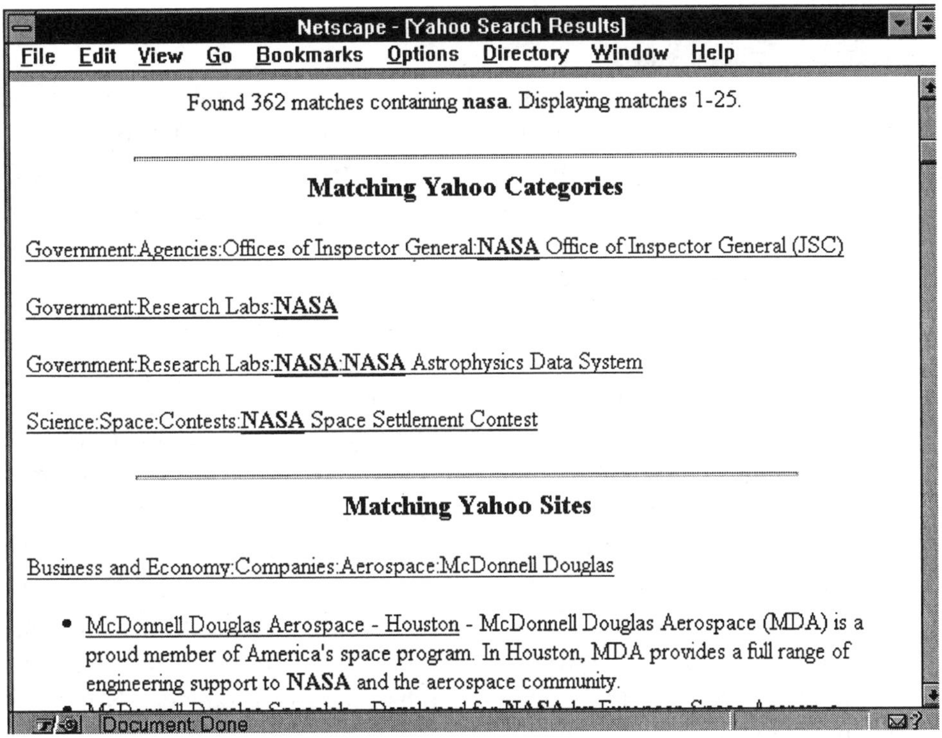

Figure 4-3

Technical Requirements for the Web

The very things that make the Web attractive make it more demanding on computer systems. Screens have attractive graphics and impressive images. Unfortunately, moving images over the Internet are much more work than moving words. Depending on the speed of your connection to the Internet, it can take seconds, or even minutes to receive a complicated Web page. If you are paying by the second and by the mile, pulling in an image from the Louvre is suddenly much less attractive. Web users tend to be people in larger universities or research centers that have flat-fee telephone arrangements. If you use the Web at home you will want the fastest modem that can run on your local phone lines.

But that raises the second problem. Full photographs can be one and two million bytes long. The local phone line that transfers 960 bytes per second (9600 baud) is going to take over one thousand seconds (17 minutes) to get the image to your computer. Suddenly flitting from Web site to Web site is a whole lot less interesting.

Capacity for high transfer rates exists in the US and most other industrial countries, or at least in some parts of these countries. The problem comes for remote businesses in the industrial world (the paper mill deep in the upper peninsula of Michigan) and for any business in the developing world. With three hundred thousand people waiting to get phones in Brazil, just getting a voice link can take months. Getting high speed data links can be impossible. Even low speed data links are difficult in Africa. As this is being written no one seems to be able to establish a data connection to Madagascar, even at 30 characters per second. At thirty characters per second it takes nearly three seconds to send one line of text and over a minute to send just one screen full of words. As for the pretty Web home page with color and graphics, a one million byte file would take nine and a half hours to transfer. Not many pretty pictures are worth a nine and a half hour wait.

If you are in one of the luckier schools that can get regular access to the World Wide Web, a group of people at the University of Minnesota is trying to keep a list of schools on the Web. Their address is:

http://web66.coled.umn.edu/schools.html#world

They can also give you a list of other schools on the web in case you wish to surf to those sites and see what other schools are doing.

Creating Your Own Web Page

Part of the reason the Web is growing so fast is that it is relatively easy to create Web pages. You can do it too. A "page" is just a word processing document that has been marked up to show how it should be displayed on the Web. These marks are part of HTML--HyperText Markup Language. What does HTML look like? Following is a small portion:

```
<!doctype html public "-//ietf//dtd html//en">
<html>
<head>
<title>Department of Mathematics and Computing, UWSP</title>
</head>
<body>
<h1 align=center >Department of Mathematics and Computing</h1>
<h1 align=center >University of Wisconsin - Stevens Point</h1>
<hr>
<h2 align=center >General Information</h2>
<p>
```
The Department of Mathematics and Computing includes majors in
Mathematics, Mathematics Education, and Computer Information
Systems. It includes 30 faculty members and roughly 400 majors.
Additional areas of research or teaching interest include Actuarial
Science, Operations Research, Secondary Education, Gender Equity, and
World Networks.
```
</p>
<p>
```
The department may be contacted via phone at
 (715) 346-
2120

Or you can reach the Department Chair, Bill Wresch,
via this email address:
bwresch@uwspmail.uwsp.edu
```
</p>
```

The words or letters in between the inequality signs (< or >) are the
commands to the Web telling it how your text should be displayed on the
screen. For instance, "h2" is the size of type--second headline. "hr" is a ruled
line across the screen. "p" is a paragraph. Figure 4-4 shows the screen that is
generated by the HTML code above.

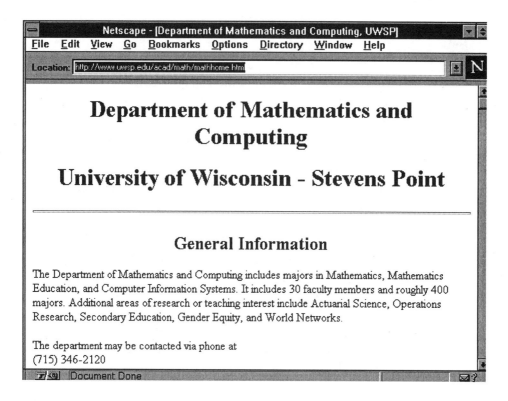

Figure 4-4

It seems confusing at first, but there aren't all that many commands and there are computer programs available that will put all the commands in for you. Where do you look for such programs? On the Web itself! Here are a few addresses to places in the Web to get help in creating your first page:

http://www.utirc.utoronto.ca/htmldocs/NewHTML/htmlindex.html
Web Index--contains a listing of resources for those creating HTML pages

http://www.utirc.utoronto.ca/htmldocs/misc_tools.html
HTML Tools--links to software to create your page

http://shu.edu/docs/about/html/html_bas.html
HTML Basics--a book on HTML

Links to these sites are also available though the course Web site.

What do you do with your document after you have created it? How does this word processing document become a Web Page? It has to be sent (usually by file transfer protocol (ftp)) to a Web server. This usually means calling up the place that is connecting you to the Internet and asking that your file reside on their computer. This is increasingly a service that comes with Internet connections. Once your page is sitting on a Web server, it has to be registered with the various search engines so they know it exists. That consists of sending an email message to Alta Vista and the rest with the URL. Now you are on the Web.

PROJECT SUGGESTIONS

🖰 Dan Gagnon and Jeff Tepp of Ben Franklin Junior High School in Stevens Point, Wisconsin give their students technology research projects on the World Wide Web. Students are supposed to find important information about technical developments. Useful sources are the home pages of computer manufacturers such as Intel or IBM. The Web is a good source of current information and gets students used to looking at professional literature. Once they have found information they are to copy the information to a computer disk and then use the information as part of a report. They are also to write valuable URL addresses on a large piece of posterboard so others in the class can see where the good sites are located.

🖰 The amount of information on the Web is so great that one good project might be to have your students create a list of URL addresses that are primary to a field. An annotated "bibliography" explaining what is to be found at each URL, and noting strengths and weaknesses, would be very valuable to other students (and maybe even to you). A few schools are beginning to create such lists and put them on the school's home page. Now if students connect to the school from home, they can get quick links to academic areas of the Web. It might also remind parents who happen to log on that your school is aware of these academic links and is actively using them.

⌐🖰   Speaking of home pages, a growing number of schools are creating a presence for themselves on the Internet through a school "homepage". This can be done fairly simply by scanning in images of your school, creating a menu of projects or events, and putting it all together using Hypertext Markup Language (HTML). The hard part of the project is less the computer skills in scanning and writing in HTML and more the selection process of deciding what should be said to the world about your school.

🖥 DISCUSSION QUESTIONS

1. What would it take for your school to get access to the World Wide Web?

2. What advantages does the Web have over email? What disadvantages?

3. By one estimate, 80% of the information on the Web is not new, but a duplicate of information--often sales literature--available elsewhere. So what is the attraction?

4. One of the attractions of the Web is its hypertext navigation system. That is also often cited as one of its weaknesses. What is the difference between hypertext and traditional organizing techniques? How do we train students to think in hypertext?

RECOMMENDED READINGS

Dern, D. *The Internet Guide for New Users.* New York: McGraw-Hill, 1994.

Kohrman, C. Let's go gophering or computers, telecommunications and the world. *ACE Newsletter,* Winter-Spring, 1995.

Richard, E. Anatomy of the World Wide Web. *Internet World,* April 1995, 28-30.

Savetz, K. The Medium is the Matrix. *Internet World,* April 1995, 70-74.

Wiggins, R. Webolution. *Internet World,* April 1995, 35-38.

Chapter 5

Classroom Management and the Net

 OVERVIEW

> *Information technology is not only changing the content of our courses, it is also changing the way we teach. Teachers using these new tools are finding themselves promoting much more cooperative learning. They are also moving more quickly to project-based learning. These and other classroom management questions will be reviewed in this chapter.*

THE MOVEMENT TO COOPERATIVE LEARNING

A social studies class is reviewing the political ads displayed in the Campaign 96 Web site. After discussing the use and misuse of political advertising, the teacher suggests a joint assignment with a English class that is currently writing argumentative papers. Students will write papers that support or attack one of the national candidates. Students with the same position meet to share evidence and help each other strengthen their arguments.

A computer studies class is teaching students how to surf the Net, and has students write their own Web pages as part of the unit. Part of each page is to be about the history of technology in America and students' perceptions of where technology will take civilization. A history teacher makes that part of the Web page an assignment in her class as well.

Interdisciplinary projects and student cooperation are hardly new in schools, but a number of forces are ensuring that joint assignments will become more common. One major force is the entire school restructuring movement. Jerry Villars sums up the reasons for this movement with his comparison of school emphases in the industrial age and the information age (Table 5-1).

Table 5-1

Industrial Age Education	Information Age Education
Top-down organization	Decentralization of decision making
Fragmented curriculum	Simplified core curriculum, interdisciplinary approaches, global emphases
Fragmented learning time	Flexible scheduling, blocks
Teacher isolation	Teams for planning and instruction
Tracking and ability grouping	Personalized instruction, groups based on task demands and interests
Students as passive consumers of information	Students as active participants in formulating and accomplishing objectives

Schools respond to changes in the communities around them, and as the workplace changes, the schoolroom will change too. We know things aren't as simplistic as the chart above would suggest (not only is much of the workplace still in the industrial age, much of it is still agricultural), but the direction is clear and our responses have already begun.

TELECOMMUNICATIONS AND
COOPERATIVE LEARNING

But the changing nature of the workplace is not the only force driving schools toward increased cooperative learning. Much of the change we are seeing is not because we *have* to change, but because we *can* change and *want* to change. Each of the upcoming chapters contains descriptions of new projects that were enabled by telecommunications. "Journey North" gives students a chance to combine science and writing and geography as they communicate with schools around the US and experts in the Arctic Circle. Email links allow students in Milwaukee do joint research on cultures with students in South Africa. Canada's Writers in Electronic Residence gives students there an audience they never had before for their writing, and new opportunities to share and discuss.

In each of these cases and many more, the power of the Internet broke down barriers of subject and nation and let students learn in exciting new ways. So teachers took advantage of the opportunity.

And there are many more examples of teachers using this new medium to promote new levels of cooperation. For now, we are not just talking about getting four or five students to work together, we are often talking about getting students in four or five countries to work together. Dan Wishnietsky tells the story of a social studies project organized by grade schools in Egypt, South America, and the US. The job of each school was to produce a student newspaper that told the story of local Thanksgiving customs. These newspapers were then exchanged electronically. Students learned that Egyptians celebrate Thanksgiving to honor Min, the god of vegetation. South American students described Thanksgiving as a celebration of the corn harvest and described the ancient use of a slave girl who dressed as a goddess, danced for a week, and was then killed. The American students pointed out that their Thanksgiving was also based around the harvest, but was celebrated somewhat differently.

In this example and in countless others, telecommunications enable a far greater amount of international, interdisciplinary cooperation.

FORMS OF COOPERATIVE LEARNING

If we are to move to more cooperative efforts in learning, what might those efforts look like? A recent publication by the National Education Association summarized five principal approaches (Table 5-2):

Table 5-2

Student Teams Achievement Division	After a teacher presents the lesson, student teams work on assignments cooperatively to master the material.
Teams, Games, Tournaments	Same as above, but after studying, students compete to win points for their team.
Jigsaw	Students each do part of a reading and then compare notes.
Learning Together	Cooperative tasks are oriented to create interdependence.
Group Investigation	Students decide what information is needed, how it will be organized, and how it will be presented.

Of the forms described by the NEA, it would appear "Group Investigation" is the approach most consonant with the kinds of projects being facilitated by telecommunications. Clearly much of the work for groups of students communicating over hundreds or thousands of miles is first deciding what information is needed. Take the Milwaukee example of students in two nations working together to determine the basics of their cultures. They are not working out of a textbook or shared group of readings. They are not listening to a teacher and then deciding how best to memorize what they have heard. They are using multiple resources--books, their teacher, the students they talk to on email. In such a system students appear more to be investigators than learners. Rather than internalizing a fixed body of information, they may begin with some principles, but then quickly expand their information sources. There is no worksheet the teacher can give them to determine whether mastery has occurred.

MAKING COOPERATIVE LEARNING WORK

While telecommunications can facilitate significant new cooperative learning opportunities, we cannot assume that these new projects will automatically be successful. We have all had group projects not work out, and adding groups from countries all over the globe may increase the potential for problems. Like any other activity, we need to think through this new form of cooperative learning and make sure we are planning as carefully as we can. A good starting point is the 11 planning steps from NEA (Lyman, 1993), as presented in Table 5-3.

Table 5-3

1. Choose your contest	"A cooperative learning strategy is chosen based on the specific objectives, student population, and grade level identified by the teacher." Since schools around the world learn different subjects at different ages than the US (especially in the areas of languages and math), choosing appropriate content for a joint investigation may take some effort.
2. Assign heterogeneous groups	"Ethnic, racial, religious, gender, academic achievement, skill ability, and other factors may be used to group students." With telecommunications, you may also be able to mix students based on country of origin. The only difficulty with international groups may be the limited access to computers both you and they may have.
3. Teach group roles	Roles may include "reader, recorder, encourager." Sensitivity to cultural differences will be important here. Many cultures have very pronounced role distinctions between males and females.

Table 5-3, *continued*

4. Assign the task	"The teacher states clearly the expectations for student learning and the purpose of the task. A time line for activities is made clear to the students." Time will be the real challenge here. Not only may it be difficult to get access to telecommunications equipment as often as you and international partners need, but foreign schools will probably be working on a different school year.
5. Move into groups	"This usually involves pushing desks closer, resulting in some noise and confusion." For telecommunications projects, moving to groups may mean moving to computers. This may create problems if the computers were set up to expect only one user at a time.
6. Give directions	"Repeat directions, and answer questions students may have at this time." If you are working with remote students, all these instructions will have to be presented via email.
7. Monitor groups	The teacher reviews group skills and facilitates problem solving as needed." As a practical matter this means having a series of "fall-back" assignments if the phone links don't work.
8. Provide closure	"The teacher collects and grades the group product." Since you may be working with teachers from other countries, you may want to talk with them first about grading customs. You may be surprised at how differently teachers around the world grade student work.
9. Evaluate the process	"In most cases students must individually demonstrate their mastery of the important skills or concepts of the learning task." The excitement of connecting to Hong Kong or South Africa should not override students' individual responsibility for mastering specific skills.
10. Maintain classroom management	"The teacher needs to encourage specific criteria for group success that add up to a well-managed classroom." You and your cooperating teachers will have to work out in advance what kinds of participation you expect from each student in a group, and monitor each group so you are sure each student is doing what you expect.
11. Plan for review	"After each lesson the teacher analyzes and reviews the lesson with the goal of improving the lesson next time it is taught." You can see how things went for your students. You will want to hear from your cooperating teachers how they perceived the lesson.

These eleven steps give helpful suggestions for making cooperative learning work in a wired classroom. One more place may be important to you --the school library. Kenneth Bruffee has some suggestions for that place.

Kenneth Bruffee has written about many aspects of cooperative learning. One of his more unexpected descriptions is of technology and new directions for libraries. He points out that libraries are less and less warehouses for books. Yes, they have books, but they also have CDs and on-line resources. These on-line resources can be documents or they can be people, and of course the people doing the accessing from the library can be individuals or groups. The result is that contemporary libraries "collect people and ideas and facilitate conversation among people." (Bruffee, 109)

He goes on to quote Joan Bechtel, "the primary task . . . of the academic library is to introduce students to the world of scholarly dialogue that spans both space and time and provide students with the knowledge and skills they need to tap into conversations on an infinite variety of topics and to participate in the . . . debate on those issues." (Bruffee, 109). We may not normally think of libraries as a place of debate, but the description actually works quite well. We all remember books we read that sparked such interest in us we felt like we were carrying on a conversation with the author. Now we not only have books as a source for that conversation over time and space, we have telecommunications terminals in the library serving as links to multiple conversations both with multiple texts and with multiple people.

Rather than being a place of silent contemplation, libraries do indeed serve more as debating halls. There may not always be shouting, but there is certainly always discussion. It is increasingly common to find library architecture rearranged to respond to this new view. Schools will place multiple chairs around a terminal so that groups of students can talk with each other as they access information and try to determine what it means. Now suddenly students are involving themselves in multiple simultaneous conversations--the local talk with their peers, the indirect talk with paper or electronic documents, the distant talk with experts or peers in other schools or other countries.

Such multiple conversations define cooperative learning in a whole new way. Yet it is an increasingly common way as more and more teachers use telecommunications for learning.

PROJECT MANAGEMENT

The model of learning described so far has three significant features. First, students take the role of explorers, going past some prescribed level of content mastery to far more substantial levels of expertise. Second, students get help in this process from their peers in their local school, from peers in distant schools, and from professionals in the field. Third, students produce products that have significant value and can be shared with audiences across the world.

That is what is possible. Now, how do we get there? Let's look at two model assignments: one using email and one using the World Wide Web. After a descritpion of each, we will review the decisions the teachers made in constructing their assignments.

Email: Jeffrey Schwartz, Fairfield, Connecticut

It is common for teachers from around the country to meet at a national conference and compare their circumstances. But with the advent of telecommunications, it is now possible for those teachers to help their students share in such meetings. One such meeting began in 1987 when Jeffrey Schwartz of the Schwickley Academy in Pennsylvania, Joanne Tulonen of Wilsall High School in Wilsall, Montana, and Bill Noll of Little Wound High School on the Pine Ridge Reservation in Kyle, South Dakota met and decided their students could learn from each other. Over the next years students wrote over 500 email messages including letters, interviews, questions, and local histories.

The first year they got acquainted with each other. Students sent personal messages, asked questions about communities, compared cultures. There were surprises. A quick question about Christmas presents made the prep school students think very differently about the situation of their new friends on the Pine Ridge Reservation. They learned about each other at a very personal level. The teachers learned too. "We were not prepared for students' limited perspectives about what it was like to grow up on a ranch in Montana or attend a prep school in Pittsburgh." (Schwartz, 1993:105). They decided to add a unit on stereotypes so students could talk through their misconceptions.

The second year the teachers moved to larger projects. Main projects included a self-portrait, an essay on the local community, and an oral history. All of these efforts were sent to the other schools in draft form, so students at the other end could ask for clarifications. These comments became so valuable that the teachers determined that all such writing should go through three exchanges so all questions could be asked and all possibilities explored. Final products were far richer because of this distant perspective.

Besides their assigned tasks, many students began reading on their own, with students in Schwickley suddenly finding the books on Native American history that had been waiting in the school library.

By the third year, each teacher had found the exchanges to be major improvements in the way students communicated and in the way students approached writing in general. They were now used to writing for an audience, used to taking an interest in the clarity and quality of their work, and wanted to write. So all three schools made email exchanges a regular part of multiple assignments. Email was totally integrated into how students wrote.

Choices

The teachers involved made a number of decisions over the years these projects evolved. Here are a few:

Who should they email? It was important to these teachers that students talk with students different from themselves. They wanted a cultural component to the conversation and carefully selected schools to achieve that end.

How should they begin? They began with personal correspondence, giving students experience with the medium. But they also watched that conversation carefully, and saw an opportunity to improve the quality of the interaction. Their movement to "stereotypes" as a focus of instruction was a signal that they would take control.

How long should this interaction last? Their decision to maintain this interaction over several years meant students would learn to trust each other, gain substantial experience, and learn at a deeper level than would have been the case over a short period of time.

What assignments should they give? These teachers took a great deal of control in the second year, moving students to specific assignments with specific processes for reviews and communication. Students might have some choice in whose oral history they would write, but they would definitely write an oral history.

In general, this period of exchanges could be characterized as very teacher-directed. Students had choices within strict confines, but the three teachers set the structure. Their educational aims were very clear, and their efforts to achieve those ends continued for years. These teachers worked very hard for their success.

WORLD WIDE WEB:
BUD DORHOLT, SHEBOYGAN HIGH SCHOOL

Bud began simply enough. His school library had access to the World Wide Web. He gave his students an introduction to the Web, let them explore, and then asked them to pick a topic for independent research. The Ebola Virus was in the news at the time and one of his students became intently interested in learning about the virus. She visited Web sites all over the world, gathering information. In two weeks she had a substantial body of research and had prepared an apparently excellent paper.

While many teachers would have simply put an A on the paper and moved on, Dorholt asked for more. He wasn't an expert on the Ebola Virus. Could she find one and ask for a review by that expert? She went back to the Web and started contacting email addresses of people who had created Web sites. Several answered, including a research physician from Denmark who had just come back from an outbreak in Zaire. He agreed to look at her paper. She sent him a copy electronically, and received a very complementary review two days later. He was astonished that a high school girl could have written a paper of such quality. She gave the email message to Dorholt, and *now* he gave her the A.

Choices

Embedded in this apparently simple assignment are a number of choices made by the teacher.

> ***What project should he assign?*** He could have given students a list of assignment topics and made them pick one. Instead he gave his students total control.

> ***What resources should they use?*** In order to make the Web manageable, some teachers are giving students specific URLs and ordering them to begin their research there. Some teachers even set up Web pages of their own, with links to resources they want students to use. Dorholt gave students total control over their searches.

> ***What level of cooperative learning should he attempt?*** It is fairly common for students to at least begin searches together, getting used to the range of options and helping each other evaluate the quality of what they find. But Dorholt had students work alone.

> ***What happens to the finished product?*** Our procedures here are pretty rote. We look at a product, grade it, and hand it back. At that point the product disappears into a backpack. Dorholt changed all that. By forcing his student to solicit professional reaction to her paper, he gave her an audience and experience in communicating with a professional in the field. Other teachers have set up school Web sites where student papers are posted. Either approach reminds us that the Web can be used to send out information, not just to receive it.

Choice Summary

As you can see from the examples above, teachers are making choices about how to structure assignments. Table 5-4 shows the summary of the choices you may want to consider.

Table 5-4

Cooperation	Will you have students work in groups? If so, will they just start a project together, or do the whole project as a group?
Assignment selection	How much freedom will you give your students? Many teachers have found lists of possible topics are a help, especially to some students.
Time	How much access to technology do you have? Does everything have to be done in two weeks? Can you give students a chance to do some casual work first? Can you create long-term connections to people around the world?
Resource selection	Will you give students lists of recommended URLs, or will you let them find their own?
Evaluation	Will you grade as usual, or will you consider the opinions of others who have read the student projects.
Product disposal	What happens when students finish? Are you able to create a Web site? Do all student papers go out on the site, or do you select?

As is always the case in schools, there are no right answers to any of these choices, just professional judgement based on your students and your circumstances. You have to decide.

Once you have created a structure for your project, you are now ready to consider the details of training your students to use the Internet. That is the focus of our next chapter.

PROJECT SUGGESTIONS

As you review the IECC Web site for international projects, notice how carefully some teachers have crafted the project they want to work on internationally. Other project ideas seem less well-formed. Contact two or three of the teachers who are named on this site and discuss their project goals. Do they already have experience with international cooperative assignments? What have they learned from the process? How have their goals changed over the years? How have their classroom management techniques changed?

🖳 DISCUSSION QUESTIONS

1. How much of your school day seems connected to "industrial age education"? How much is "information age"?

2. Which forms of cooperative learning have you tried? Which work best for telecommunications projects?

3. Of the 11 steps in cooperative learning presented by the NEA, which do you see as most difficult in international projects?

4. If you were initiating an Internet project with your students this year, what choices would you make about the structure of the project?

RECOMMENDED READING

Adams, D., Carlson, H., and Hamm, M. (1990). *Cooperative Learning and Educational Media: Collaborating with Technology and Each Other.* Englewood Cliffs, NJ: Educational Technology Publications.

Bruffee, K. A. (1993). *Collaborative Learning: Higher Education, Interdependence, and the Authority of Knowledge.* Baltimore, MD: The Johns Hopkins University Press.

Frick, T. W. (1991). *Restructuring Education through Technology.* Bloomington, IN: Phi Delta Kappa Educational Foundation.

Hilke, E. V. (1990). *Cooperative Learning.* Bloomington, IN: Phi Delta Kappa Educational Foundation.

Layman, L., Foyle, H. C., and Azwell, T. S. (1993). *Cooperative Learning in the Elementary Classroom.* National Education Association.

Monroe, R. (1993). *Writing and Thinking with Computers.* Urbana, IL: National Council of Teachers of English.

Schwartz, J. (1991). Writing Exchanges on an Electronic Network. 104-108. In Wresch, W. (Ed.), *The English Classroom in the Computer Age: Thirty Lesson Plans.* Urbana, IL: National Council of Teachers of English.

Villars, J. (1991). *Restructuring through School Redesign.* Bloomington, IN: Phi Delta Kappa Educational Foundation.

Wishnietsky, D. H. (1993). *Using Computer Technology to Create a Global Classroom.* Bloomington, IN: Phi Delta Kappa Educational Foundation.

Wresch, W. (1993). *The English Classroom in the Computer Age: Thirty Lesson Plans.* Urbana, IL: National Council of Teachers of English.

Chapter 6
Introducing Students to the Net

⌨ OVERVIEW

A basic question for teachers is "how do I present this to my students?" What topics should I include? How much detail should I use? What materials should they see? A particular question for the Internet is procedural versus topical information. Do I just teach them how to use the Internet, or do I also teach them about the Internet as a subject?

GENERAL PREPARATION FOR STUDENTS

One of the first choices we have with using telecommunications is how much we actually want our students to see. Elementary school teachers regularly hide virtually the entire process from their younger students, using adult volunteers to type in messages and send them out. Meanwhile in many high schools, students are expected to run the entire process from logging on to downloading files.

Maybe a good way to start is to list the skills that telecommunications requires. We will look at each and let teachers decide for themselves whether their students are ready to perform these tasks unaided.

Keyboarding

It is now common for students in third and fourth grade to receive some instruction in touch typing. But using a computer is more than learning basic typing. Students have to be able to find some of the specialized computer keys. For email it is crucial that they be able to find the @ character. They also have to understand that spaces (and lack of spaces) are important. If they send a message to me at this address:

bwresch@fsmail.uwsp.edu

the message will arrive. If they add just one space, like this address

bwresch @fsmail.uwsp.edu

the message will **not** arrive. Typing email addresses may require more attention to detail than young students are ready for. For that reason, many teachers have their young students type the message, but parent volunteers (or librarians) type in the email addresses.

Network Connections

Establishing a link between an individual computer and the network that will carry email traffic can vary from the simple to the complex. Professional networks like America Online supply software that creates a simple interface on the screen and does most of the work for users. University networks tend to be much more complicated. You may need to know a particular phone number and answer a series of questions about your machine so the university computer can arrange your screen in a readable manner.

The real problem may be that each network has its own command sequence, so students may have tobe taught several different programs and sequences. And of course all of these sequences are changing as networks upgrade their programs and you reach out to use newer systems.

Whatever system you use, the network will require that students be capable of following a specific set of instructions and that they do every step without fail. You may be surprised at how much trouble some of your brighter students get into since they may be used to taking shortcuts and doing things their own way. Network connections are not forgiving.

Navigation

Once students have made their electronic connection and are on-line, they need to be able to travel around in the virtual world. This means being able to move through menus, work through hypertext, and somehow get back to where they started so they can exit cleanly. Students who can't navigate a system create two problems. First, they never find the information they were looking for. Second, it is fairly common for confused students to just shut off a computer rather than exit from a program. Without a normal exit, the network itself can become confused about who is connected, and the system may continue charging for a connection or may leave an entry point tied up even though it is no longer in use.

One way to begin a lecture on navigation is to show students how to leave. This may seem an odd way to begin, but it is much like Hansel and Gretel and the bread crumbs. The forest is much less threatening if you are sure you can get back out. How do you leave? For the World Wide Web there is the home icon, for Gopher there is the escape key, and for most libraries there is a special function key. For each system there is a way to return to the beginning. The example below from Keypals provides an illustration of most of the common navigational tools available on-line.

> *Notice first the control boxes:*
> *Back*
> *Forward*
> *Home*
> *They are located at the top of the screen and so are easy to find.*

There are two other navigation approaches shown on the screen (see Figure 6-1). The first is the line for the URL or address. By typing in a particular address, you can get the program to jump to that new Web site. The other navigation approach is buried in the underlined text. All of these are hypertext links and will take the student to related materials.

The World Wide Web demonstrates just how sophisticated navigational strategies have become. Unfortunately, students will need to know about other navigational approaches since each program takes its own approach. And unfortunately, most approaches are less sophisticated.

Figure 6-1

How do you get students ready to move comfortably around such programs? Much comes just from general computer experience. Many of our students are using computers enough at home, and so moving around the Web or Gopher offers no challenge at all. Other students are less lucky. For them, you may want to create road maps for each program. Experience with good hypertext software can also be helpful. In general, computer interface designers are coming to agree on a standard interface that looks much like the screens of the World Wide Web.

Storage Concepts

They are reading an article on their screen. Where is that article? It may be sitting on a computer thousands of miles away. It may be in their own computer's dynamic memory. It may be sitting on a CD-ROM in the library. Does it matter? Not while they are reading. But what if they want to include a paragraph or two from that article in their research paper? They need to make a copy of those paragraphs and transfer them to a disk in their own computer. Now storage matters.

Almost every program has a way of copying portions of articles. Students may need to copy files or to use a "clip board" to copy and paste interesting sections of articles. Ultimately, copies of text have to be moved onto a floppy disk in the student's own computer. Students need to know how to do that, as well as how to check to be sure the document they *think* they saved was really saved. A good background for this is just general word processing practice.

Information Concepts

While using software is important, the real reason we have students use telecommunications is to gain information. They need to know some information concepts as well. While you will already have taught them about basic concepts, electronic text provides two new problems. One is integrity and the other is authority.

College students all over America now have their own personal Web pages, and include copies of their old term papers. They have become an information resource. It is great that students are willing to share their research. But there is nothing to prevent unscrupulous students from "borrowing" all kinds of papers sitting out on the Web. They can be easily copied to any word processor, slightly changed, and turned in as the student's own. One solution is to recast assignments as I-Search papers where students include a narrative of what they found where and how they conducted their research. But clearly we have even more opportunities for plagiarism than existed before.

The second issue is authority. In the past we knew who experts were-- they were the people who had books in the library. But now the Web is filled with the latest ideas of experts, and the latest ravings by every crackpot in the nation. Both sit next to each other on the Web and may appear equally professional, complete with nicely scanned images. How do you tell your students which ideas should be taken seriously? They need to find signs of authority--connections to a university or professional organization, listings of more traditional publications, some sign that the person has legitimate expertise.

Katrina Beard, a teacher in Australia, offers this checklist as a way of validating information your students find on the Internet:

1. Who put this information here? The source of the material might give you a clue to its reliability. A site maintained by a university or government organization might be more reliable than one maintained by a private citizen.

2. How old is the material? Sometimes the age of information matters. If you need current statistics then check the age of the material you have found. As a rule of thumb, in most fields anything more than five years old is probably outdated. This doesn't mean that you shouldn't use it, but you need to be aware that your information is not necessarily the most recent.

3. How often is the site updated? Again, if you need recent material it is important that the site you are using is updated regularly.

4. Who wrote the information? The status of the writer is often of considerable importance in deciding the reliability of material on the Net. You can probably assume that material written or otherwise provided by a known expert in the field is likely to be reliable. If you have never heard of the writer do some research on him or her. Check a Dictionary of Biography or a Who's Who.

5. Why is this material here? Who put the material on the Internet and why? Think about whether they might have some reason other than pure helpfulness for posting information. Many special interest groups have Web pages, and while this doesn't necessarily mean the material is biased it is something you need to think about.

6. Can I do a cross check? Think about ways you might cross check the information you have found. You might have a look at another site with similar material, ask somebody who knows something about the topic, have a look at books on the subject. Use your own experience as well. If you have already done some research in the area you will already have some knowledge of the subject. How does this material fit in with what you already know?

The problem of authority of information is so significant, some schools are moving toward "Information Literacy" as a skill they teach and test. By this they usually mean the ability to find information, evaluate it, and present it. All three matter. In the past we had librarians teach information access, and English teachers teach information presentation. Little was said about information evaluation because it was assumed the school librarian had solved most of that problem through careful selection of books and periodicals. Once students get on the Internet and leave the school library, evaluation is a huge problem and a skill that must be taught.

URL Citations

Once students find information on the Internet, they need to know how to cite these resources. There is a Web page with the details of this process:

http://www.classroom.net/classroom/CitingNetResources.htm

In general, the approach is to include this information:

1. **Author** (if known). What person or group created the page?
2. **Title of the page.**
3. **URL**
4. **Date visited** (pages change so fast, the date is necessary to help identify what might have been found there.)

Searching

This is a special problem worth a great deal of thought. We know the Internet is growing at an amazing rate. This is one of its strengths. But it is also one of its problems. How do you find things on the Internet when there are thousands of new entries each day? The response has been to create "search engines," programs that find materials for you. There is only one problem--each search engine uses a slightly different strategy, so that doing the same search on two different programs may return two totally different results.

Let me demonstrate with a model search on a subject of interest to all of us --teacher's salaries. In the first case I will use one popular search engine-- WebCrawler. As you can see in Figure 6-2, it gives me a list of pages related to the topic of teacher's salaries. My next job will be to select each of those pages in turn to see if any actually contain information that might be of use to me.

WebCrawler does a "key word" search. How can it do such a search? It has to be told by authors what their Web pages are about. It then looks through a table of topics it maintains and prints out pages that meet the subject you request.

There are other ways of doing a search. For instance, libraries not only let you do subject searches, but they also group books around similar subjects, so you can often find what you want just by browsing down the right aisle. This

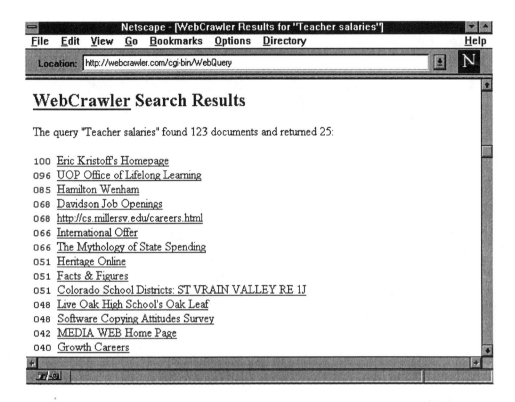

Figure 6-2

technique is also available electronically. The program that uses it is called Yahoo. Two screens illustrating its search technique are shown in Figures 6-3 and 6-4.

Notice that I now have two strategies--I can use a key word search, or go directly to a subject and browse. Here are the results of a key word search (Figure 6-4). Notice that it runs up different results than WebCrawler.

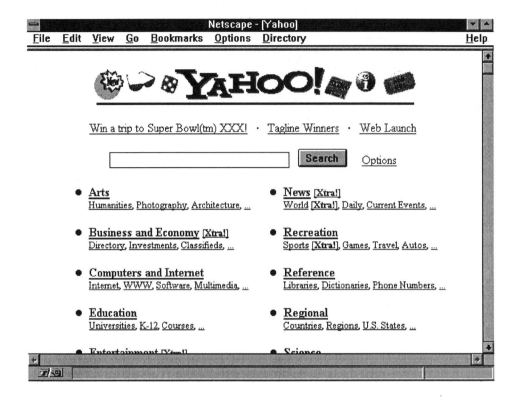

Figure 6-3

Each search engine finds resources for me, but I have to know to use both (or more) to really find all that is out there. It is like we are dealing with a library with dozens of different card catalogs in the lobby. Using one will tell you about some of the books, another will tell you about different books. As of now, there is no catalog that will tell you about all books.

Besides identifying which search program to use, students will also have to know about Boolean operators used to limit searches. The possibilities are presented in Table 6-1.

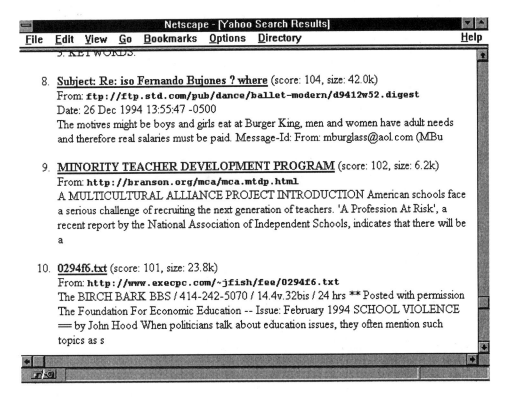

Figure 6-4

Table 6-1   Boolean operators

AND	Search: **Teachers AND salaries** (Only show me sites that mention both)
OR	Search: **Teachers OR salaries** (Show me all sites that mention EITHER teachers OR salaries)
NOT	Search: **Teachers NOT salaries** (Show me sites that describe anything to do with teachers EXCEPT salaries)

As you can see, those three little words would make a huge difference in the number of Web sites that would be listed after each of the searches. In general, students want AND as a way of controlling the number of sites they will have to look through.

PROJECT SUGGESTIONS

🖱 The Silence Project is a Web site that tracks information silences around the world. Its address is

http://www.uwsp.edu/acad/math/silence.html

Have students read through the pages of the "Silence Map" to familiarize themselves with where information is available and where it is not (Figure 6-5). They should quickly begin to see the major issues involved. Also have them read through the materials developed by the Canadian government (under "Groups that Help") to defend and promote its culture in the face of US dominance in the information field.

After they have reviewed the issues and the responses, have your students look through the Web on their own. Can they identify empty places on the net? Groups not heard from? For example, General Motors has an extensive Web presence to sell its cars. Is there an equivalent presence of GM's unions? Of consumers? What sides of arguments aren't being presented on the Web?

🖱 Another very valuable project would be to create a manual for your students. What assignments would you give them to build their understanding of telecommunications? What handouts would you create? What decisions would you make about what they should do and what adults should do?

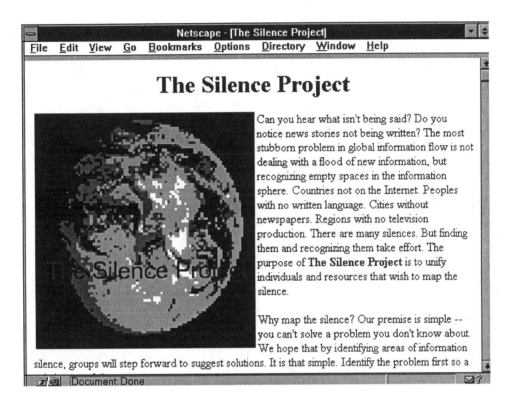

Figure 6-5

🖰 Pick a research subject and have students do a comparison of sources. For instance, if they were to look at Ford Motor Company, what information might they get on the World Wide Web? What information from a periodical CD? What information from books in your library? A comparison might help them temper their enthusiasm for all things electronic, and could help persuade them that they need to consider many sources when doing research.

Another way to help educate students about the wide range of sources in the Internet would be to pick three sites. One would be obviously biased (a political or commercial site advertising a candidate or product), one would be impartial but not well informed (an amateur's attempt to produce their own Buyer's Guide), and the third would be a more professional resource. Ask students to identify signs that show one site to be more valid than the others.

DISCUSSION QUESTIONS

1. Have you ever been lost on the information highway? How did you stop for directions?

2. Can we agree on what students can do at certain ages?

3. What kinds of computer activities provide good background for telecommunications work?

4. Are you encountering student plagiarism? What do you do about it?

5. The Web is very democratic--experts and novices can present ideas side by side. What are the advantages of that? The dangers?

6. What tips do you give students when they start doing on-line searches? Do you screen topics first?

Chapter 7
Curriculum Integration: Science and Math

 ## OVERVIEW

For science teachers the Internet has been an exciting opportunity to connect students to real science. A number of projects have been created to make such connections easier. The challenge for math teachers is to both teach math and to convince students that math matters. There are plenty of Internet sites to help with both.

FOUR BENEFITS OF THE INTERNET

There are a number of good sources of scientific and mathematics information available on the Internet. One way to think about these sources is to look at their direct benefit to students. From that perspective, the sources seem to fall into four broad categories.

Access to Real Data

We know we want to give students experience with the surprises of science, and so we have them perform experiments. But there are practical problems--safety, cost, availability. We end up with very limited experiments that too often look more like a cooking class in that all the ingredients are mixed in prescribed amounts and the end result is an expected outcome. There isn't much mystery or excitement.

For students to experience real science, they need access to more data, to real observations rather than numbers pulled from a lab manual. From time to time, they also need to deal with numbers that just don't make sense--false readings or unexpected phenomena. Experience with real data can begin at an early age. One of the principles of KidsNet is that elementary school students should have some opportunities to collect data, share it with others, and form conclusions from the data they receive. In one exchange, students collect information about pets and send it to other classrooms on the Net. Students then graph out the kinds of pets that are found around the country looking for patterns. Such activities may not be "science" in the way we usually think of it, but this is actually a good way for young students to gather data and try to make sense of it--the heart of science.

Dick Upton's middle school students in Platteville, Wisconsin connected to a project called "Journey North," in which a group of arctic explorers send back data they gathered as they crossed to the North Pole. They tagged a number of migrating animals, and let schools collect data from radio collars. One of the more interesting moments came as one of the signals remained stationary for days. The event was unpredictable and left students wondering whether they were looking at broken equipment or a dead animal. There was no way of being sure, so students were introduced to the inherent uncertainties of science.

Access to Professional Journals

We too often overlook the fact that mathematicians and scientists have access to a significant body of published research. They begin with an ability to read the work that has gone on before. We, on the other hand, have to work with the general purpose magazines in the typical school library, magazines that are simply not directed at real scientific research.

Linda Trzebiatowski of the Rosholt, Wisconsin Public Schools is one of a growing number of teachers who have turned to electronic links to solve that problem. She has each of her high school students write a paper on a health-related topic. To ensure that they can find articles that are both current and sufficient in number, she has had her library install a series of CD-ROMs. CDs can hold thousands of articles in very little space, and have the added advantage of being searchable by key word. Now students can do the kind of searching they would do with a card catalog, with two key additions:

1. The first response to any search is the number of items available. This helps students get a sense of the scope of their subject. If they have picked something as vague as "AIDS", they can expect to see hundreds of articles. It is an early warning that they need to narrow their scope.

2. Once they have identified an appropriate subject, they can be assured that they will actually get to read the articles they find. There is nothing more disappointing that starting a search only to find that most of the materials you need are unavailable. You have the title and the author, but the magazine is not in your library. An increasing number of CDs contain the entire text of the article right on the CD so you can jump right to any article you find.

One last help Linda Trzebiatowski has for her students is a list of topics she recommends. Her better students will gravitate to good topics on their own. For weaker students, however, she has a list of topics she has checked out herself. She knows the number of articles available is reasonable for them, and that some of the articles are in popular journals that will be easier for these students to read.

Besides CDs, students can also access professional data through both the World Wide Web and Gopher. Good places to start are your own professional organizations. Both the National Council of Teachers of Mathematics and the

National Science Teacher's Association maintain their own Web pages. While these sites are primarily intended for teachers, they are beginning to build links to classroom projects and to online resources. These are what those two sites look like (Figures 7-1 and 7-2):

http://www.nctm.org -- National Council of Teachers of Mathematics

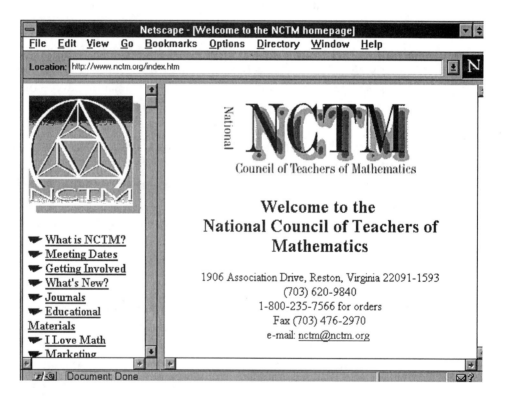

Figure 7-1

http://www.nsta.org -- National Science Teacher's Association

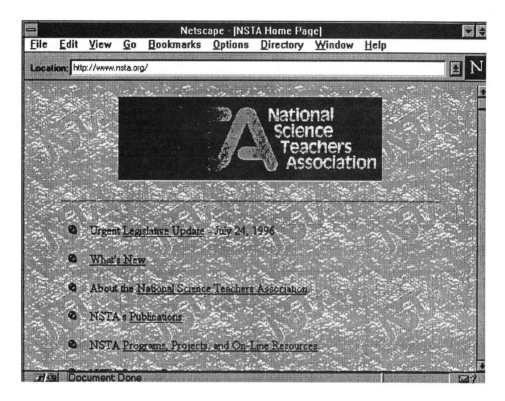

Figure 7-2

Access to Experts

Textbooks are very good at telling us about science of the past. Where do we keep up to date with current developments in science and math? We may read in newspapers or magazines about major projects: How could we make contact with some of those scientists? How do we link our students to real living, breathing scientists? To active mathematicians? Here we are lucky since a number of agencies have made their experts available to students. Who's on-line? Here are a few resources:

Women of NASA
http://quest.arc.nasa.gov/women/hpage.html

NASA has created this web site as a way of introducing students to the day to day working reality of female scientists. A dozen or so younger women describe how they became interested in science, the schooling they went through, problems they overcame, and what they do now at NASA. Here are a couple of screens that illustrate the nature of this resource (Figures 7-3 and 7-4):

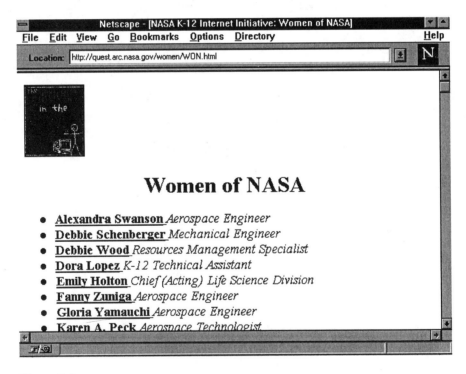

Figure 7-3

For each woman there is an entry with picture and academic background. Here is a typical example:

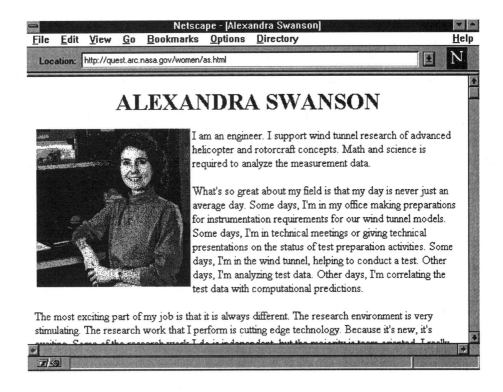

Figure 7-4

It was originally expected that students could write to these women with questions about their activities, but budget cuts have reduced those options. Maybe in the future.

Scientist on Tap
scientist-on-tap@gsn.org

Scientists at California's Jet Propulsion Laboratory describe research they are doing. Students are able to ask questions and learn about JPL's projects.

Ask a Geologist
ask-a-geologist@usgs.gov

Have a question about earthquakes? Scientists at the US Geological Survey will take them.

Jane Goodall Institute
jg@gsn.org

Here is a good source of information about environmental issues, and a chance to talk with some of the leading natural scientists in the world.

The Jason Project
http://seawifs.gsfc.nasa.gov/jason/html/jason_home.html

This is a Web page describing the current explorations of the Jason project. Participants join participating scientists during actual research projects.

Ask Dr. Math
http://forum.swarthmore.edu/dr.math/abt.drmath.html

Here is a way for students to get their questions about mathematics answered.

Math Magic
http://forum.swarthmore.edu/mathmagic/what.html

This site was set up to encourage problem solving and communication skills in math. New opportunities are being created all the time. A good source to stay current on such projects is the Global Schoolhouse (**http://gsn.org/gsn/gsn.projects.html**). Their Web page is updated regularly to include emerging projects.

The point of all these projects is to give your students a chance to talk electronically with professionals in science and math. The hope of agencies like NASA and JPL is that once the average student learns more about what scientists really do, even if they don't become professional scientists, they will be more aware of the excitement of science.

Opportunities to Do Real Science

Science makes a poor spectator sport. Dick Upton's middle school students in Platteville, Wisconsin began by reading the reports being sent down to them by arctic explorers. That was nice for a while, but it left the students watching science instead of doing science. Dick's response was to ask his students to begin making guesses about what information would come their way. Could they predict the migration paths of caribou? They got out the maps and recorded the paths and made their guesses.

Once started, they began contacting other schools by email, seeing what hypotheses they had made. This led them to butterfly migration--when would butterflies make the northward trek to Platteville? They read about butterflies, checked with schools in the southern US, and guessed at temperatures that would be needed before butterflies would venture north. With other schools on-line to give them progress reports, three Platteville students were able to predict to the day when the butterflies would arrive.

This ability to ask questions, make predictions, share results, and test hypotheses has always been possible in a local environment, but now electronic communications means that students have access to far more data in more interesting places. In short, doing science can be more fun now.

PROJECT SUGGESTIONS

The scientists available on-line have many things to tell students, but then so do books. One of the first issues for students will be deciding which questions should be asked of real scientists and which should be learned the old fashioned way. For instance, it would seem a waste of time to dial up the Jet Propulsion Laboratory just to ask the distance of the sun from the earth. Similarly, Ask Dr. Math seems a poor place to send in homework problems. Clearly such expertise should be used for enrichment activities. A good project would be to begin framing the proper relationship among your class, your on-line experts, and your library.   Could you create a research project that correctly coordinated all three?

NASA puts a great deal of effort into developing lesson plans that coordinate with shuttle launches and other major events. You might download their materials and develop a unit around such a launch.

There is a personal side to science. With access to a number of working scientists, you might have students begin collecting answers to such questions as, Why did you become a scientist? What is a typical day like? What is the worst part of your job? When did you know you wanted to be a scientist?

The danger of connecting students to practicing scientists is that students may feel overwhelmed. Here are these scientists doing all this exciting stuff, and here they are going to school--same old, same old. A valuable project would be to develop extensions that could be accomplished by students themselves. Dick Upton's idea of tracking butterflies after seeing scientists track caribou would be a good model. What can students do now? How can they learn to see themselves as scientists even at this young age?

🖥 DISCUSSION QUESTIONS

1. There are many Web sites available with science project ideas. One you might start with is Newton's Apple (**http://www.mnonline.org/ktca/newtons/alpha.html**). It provides project suggestions to go with each of its television shows. A sample lesson follows:

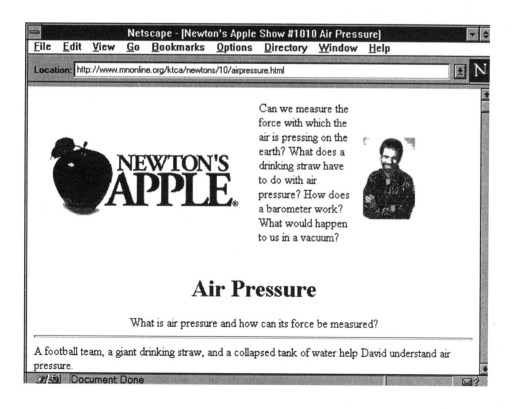

Netscape - [Newton's Apple Show #1010 Air Pressure]

File Edit View Go Bookmarks Options Directory Window Help

Location: http://www.mnonline.org/ktca/newtons/10/airpressure.html

Can we measure the force with which the air is pressing on the earth? What does a drinking straw have to do with air pressure? How does a barometer work? What would happen to us in a vacuum?

Air Pressure

What is air pressure and how can its force be measured?

A football team, a giant drinking straw, and a collapsed tank of water help David understand air pressure.

Document Done

Review several of these lessons. How would you evaluate the quality of the materials they are presenting? Have several of your students review these sites. How engaging do they find the materials?

2. How do you balance large-scale projects and the normal curriculum? Can the two coexist?

3. What are the biggest needs in the current science curriculum. Which are being met by these on-line resources? Which are not?

4. What can these practicing scientists tell your students about mathematics? Have your students ask at least three scientists how they use algebra.

5. Some of the math projects involve telecommunications as a way to get students to write more about math. Could you explain to a parent why writing about math is worth the effort to get a class on-line?

Chapter 8
Curriculum Integration:
Social Science

 OVERVIEW

For teachers trying to help students gain a better understanding of their world, telecommunications can be a direct connection to current events and world cultures. If the world is in fact getting smaller, we need our students to have a much better understanding of different places and cultures. Telecommunications can be a link to that smaller world.

COMMON APPROACHES

There is a growing appreciation for all students to know more about the world --its geography, its history, its peoples and their cultures. Even relatively small American businesses sell internationally, while the advanced countries of the world build assembly plants across America. How can we prepare students to know more about other countries? Teachers who have been able to get phone lines into their classrooms have been able to invent many new strategies, but these main themes predominate.

People to People

John Thompson's eighth grade classroom in Milwaukee, Wisconsin demonstrates this approach quite well. He spent hours making email connections around the world until he found a teacher in Mamelodi, South Africa who had similar interests. Once they found each other, they planned a series of activities that would let their students interact directly. John and his South African peer framed the discussion as a cultural exchange. What are the major daily experiences of people across the world? They had students take a look at their own cultures--housing, schooling, clothing, recreations--and then send a description of that daily life to peers across the world.

To facilitate exchanges, students were paired up and wrote to each other several times. The hope was that once students got to know each other, dialogue would be easier, and might lead to deeper discussion of daily life. Much of that seems to have happened. Email connectivity in South Africa is more limited than in the US, so responses took several days, but students were able to connect directly to a student like themselves and compare the basic elements of their daily lives.

As is often the case, students found they had much more in common than they had thought. Reared on movies that make Africa appear to be nothing but a backdrop to Tarzan adventures, American students were surprised to learn that their peers in Mamelodi wore shoes, lived in houses, and took the train to school. In short, in many ways their lives were like the lives students in Milwaukee were living. Unfortunately, both groups also found they were afraid of all the guns in their communities and wanted to move away from all the violence.

In some sense, this approach to telecommunications simply builds on the old penpal technique of helping students learn directly about the world person to person. The key advantage is time. Rather than waiting weeks for letters to make the round trip, students need wait only a few days. For connections to the developed parts of the world, the round trip can take just hours. This is not just a matter of convenience. With responses arriving more quickly, student interest stays higher and more communication can occur. It appeared in John Thompson's classroom that several of the students had developed real attachments to their peers in Africa. They felt like they knew the person they were writing to and were moving beyond the minimum requirements of assignments to more elaborate and detailed exchanges. They were building an interest in Africa and learning much more about life there from this approach than they would have from textbooks.

How can you make these connections? While informal "surfing" will eventually connect you with peers who share your interests, you can also turn to organized forums for classes. We have already mentioned the Intercultural E-Mail Classroom Connections (**http://www.stolaf.edu/network/iecc/**) as a good starting point for finding connected classrooms around the world. Another interesting approach comes from the Global School House project. Their global grocery list is an easy way for your students to study world costs for common items. Your students go into local stores and get local prices for items on a common list. They send those prices in for your community and find out what similar items cost in countries around the world. The address for that project is:

ggl-L@gsn.org

A large number of schools around the world are creating their own Web pages. These pages are also a good way to make contact. One interesting guide to these pages comes from the Western Cape School Network in South Africa (Figure 8-1). Its Web address is:

http://www.wcape.school.za

As more and more nations put their schools onto the World Wide Web, it will be easier for your students to see what their peers around the world are doing.

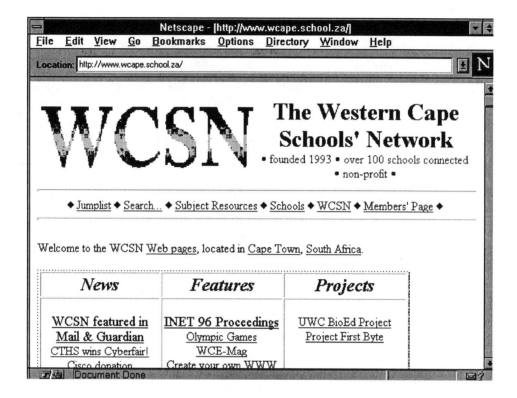

Figure 8-1

Students to Experts

For Jim Gryleski of Rosholt, Wisconsin, an Internet connection was an opportunity to connect his students to experts around the world. One of his first connections was to a woman at a UN relief agency in Switzerland. She was happy to tell his students about relief efforts around the world, and to give them the latest information about various events around the world. One of her projects was in Rwanda and she was able to tell students in Rosholt, Wisconsin details of refugee life that were unavailable to professional journalists.

Jim's next activity was to link his students to his brother in Hong Kong. He felt there were two main advantages to this connection. The first was that his brother was just a "normal guy." He was a Wisconsin boy who had gone to a Wisconsin college and then taken a job in business. Just a few years out of college, the business had sent him to Hong Kong to live and work. The lesson for Jim's students was that overseas travel was not just for the rich and famous but for ordinary people like themselves. The second advantage of this connection was that they had a very patient correspondent, one who would write each week with details of life such as the cost of an apartment, the contents of a meal, the commute to work. Questions that interested students but were unanswerable through textbooks (like "What is your apartment like?") could be answered in hours.

What is striking about these electronic connections is how many experts are willing to take the time to speak electronically to children. Part of the answer lies in the advantages of electronic conversations. Experts don't need to find time to travel to schools, and can answer their mail anytime during the night or day when they have time--electronic communication is convenient. But part of the answer seems to be that many adults are simply generous with their time--willing to help kids despite all the other demands that they may face.

Students to World Resources

While having direct access to people around the world is important, there are other important resources. Many nations are setting up Web pages that provide geographic, economic, and cultural data. They may also list current events and have links to local companies and national newspapers. In short, they can provide much more information than may be available in a typical geography textbook. Figure 8-2 shows an example of one such national page.

Such national pages are a great source of current news, but they are created by the local government. For a more unbiased (and often more interesting) view of the world, a good source is on-line newspapers. A growing number of newspapers are putting their issues on-line and making them available all over the world. One of the better African newspapers is the

Weekly Mail and Guardian of South Africa. Figure 8-3 shows what it makes available over the Internet.

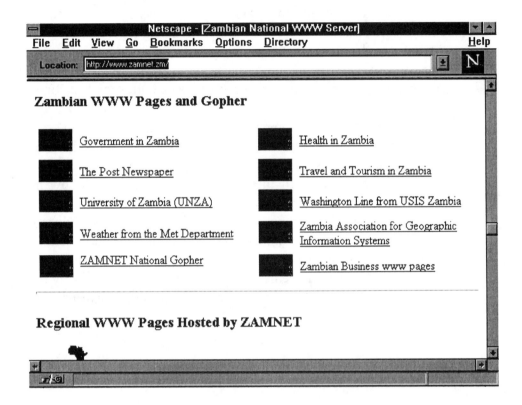

Figure 8-2

In addition to giving an overview of current stories, the Weekly Mail and Guardian also has a search program built into its page, so students who want to look at all stories published on schools or elections can download every story that has appeared in the paper.

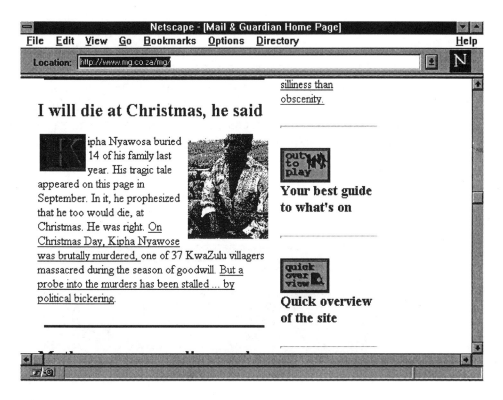

Figure 8-3

Students to National Resources

While you travel the world, don't forget the US. Most states now have Web pages and Gopher sites with information about current legislation and economic activity. Congress now has its own site too, Thomas. This is a complete listing of bills before Congress and all legislative activity. Its address is:

http://thomas.loc.gov

Thomas has several ways of accessing current legislation. It has headings by topic and a search tool so that you can search for all current legislation connected to the environment, for example, or higher education. Besides legislation, Thomas also has a searchable copy of the Congressional Record, so you can read what has been said on the Senate floor. That in itself can be an education. The following screens show first the main Thomas screen (Figure 8-4), and then the results of a search on the topic "Universities" (Figure 8-5).

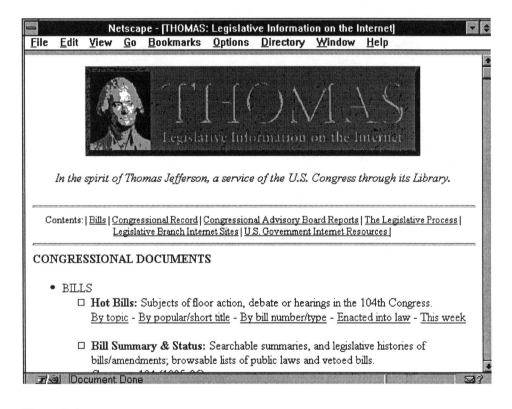

Figure 8-4

As you can see, much of the Congressional Record shows not weighty deliberations over matters of great substance, but congratulations over anniversaries and success on the basketball court.

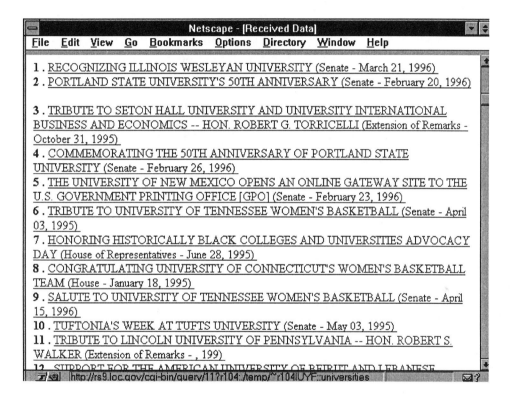

Figure 8-5

The complete text of each section can be obtained just by clicking on the appropriate portion of the screen (and you too can read a tribute to the Tennessee Women's basketball team).

Congress isn't the only government site on the web. You can get to most federal government Web pages by using **http://www.fedworld.gov**

Students to Current Events

There are a growing number of national and international sites for news and current events. Many newspapers are now on the Web, although many have a delay between when they print their paper and when they put news on the Web. Papers seem uncertain about how much they want to support the Web, since it is a competitor, but for the moment a great deal of news is available over the Internet. Try these sites for starters:

> **http://www.yahoo.com/headlines**
> **http://www.yahoo.com/News/Current_Events/**
> **http://www.web500.com/categories/Current_Events/current.htm**
> **http://campaign.96.com**
> **http://www.chicago.tribune.com/**
> **http://www.nytimes.com**

Students to Historical Resources

In addition to current affairs and international events, the Web also has access to important historical archives that might not be included in your local library. Many more are listed at the back of this book, but here are a few to start:

> *United States Holocaust Museum*
> **http://www.ushmn.org**
>
> *Civil War*
> **http://cobweb.utcc.utk.edu/~hoemann/warweb.html**
> **http://www.ucsc.edu/civil-war-letters/**

Curriculum Integration Suggestions

The Internet gives us marvelous opportunities to speak directly to people around the world, to tap expertise not normally available to our classrooms, and to access materials we might only have dreamed of before. But we still need some way to connect these new materials with the existing curriculum. It will be years before we are as comfortable with this new information source as we are with textbooks and movies, but there are three issues we should face immediately.

The first problem is time. For most teachers, the clock has thirty six weeks in it and it runs unmercifully. One extra week spent on one area means one week less somewhere else. This can quickly become a problem with email projects. You have set aside three weeks for Africa, but the email connections are bringing in great information and students have built relationships that they (and you) feel uncomfortable dropping. But if you add two more weeks to Africa, you need to take two weeks from the Middle East. That doesn't seem fair either. So what do you do?

Actually this is just another version of the old depth versus breadth decision. Do you concentrate on just a few areas and have students learn them really well, or do you adopt the "If this is Tuesday it must be Belgium" approach? The choice is, of course, yours. But you should begin any use of email knowing that it will extend the time you normally give to that unit.

The second problem is reading. If you have reluctant readers (is there anybody who doesn't?), you may find that they stop reading the textbook entirely. After all, in their minds, why read, when you can just send a message electronically and find out anything you want? The solution here is easy. You can assign the chapter in the textbook (and test their knowledge) before they get on-line. Among other things, this means that students engage in much more substantial conversations when they get on-line. After all, what sense does it make to establish a cross-world electronic link only to have students ask, "Where is Hong Kong?"

John Thompson's approach is to have students write all their messages on a word processor before they go on-line, and he grades the messages as he would any other assignment. Other teachers have students do research using normal classroom materials before they begin asking for information on-line. In either case, the point is to remind students that reading is still an important skill and the textbook still has a purpose.

The third problem is really an opportunity to motivate. While we have been talking about email as a source of information and a way for students to find out about the world, it can also be a place for students to publish their work.   What better way for students to determine how well they really understand a country than to have them write a paper on a country and then email it to a peer in that country? "Here is what I said about Germany. Is it right?" It is a great motivator to get it right.

By way of illustration, a couple years back a rather proud young man wrote an essay in which he praised the Greeks as the founders of modern civilization. He then electronically sent the essay off to a group of other schools. A day later he got an email message from Hong Kong saying, "The Greeks did all this **when**? You might want to read a paragraph or two of Chinese history and compare dates." The proud young man didn't need to read much Chinese history to realize he had much more to learn about the world.

PROJECT SUGGESTIONS

⌐ If you have email capability, use the St. Olaf resource to find a school that matches your interests. Create a unit plan with these materials: What should students know about that country before you begin electronic exchanges? What do you want them to learn? What will they do with what they learn? Will it be on a test, or part of a research report? What can they learn electronically that can't be learned through available library resources? What library resources should they be using at the same time?

⌐ Visit any university library that has access to the World Wide Web, and do research yourself on some country you plan to cover this year. Search government sources, business sources, and local newspapers. What can you learn about the country that is important for your students? All the materials you bring to your computer screen can be printed off. Print those that you would share with your class. How will you merge this new material with what you normally use?

⌐ "Thomas" is a great way to learn about the American government. See if you can determine what topics draw the most attention in Congress. Which draw the least? Collect materials that would help your class get a better understanding of how Congress actually operates.

🖳 DISCUSSION QUESTIONS

1. If you are already connected to a foreign school, how did you make that connection and what did you discuss on-line?

2. Can we create a list of questions we might ask of foreign students? What would we want students to know before they get on-line?

3. Which countries have the best Web sites?

4. What agencies other than Congress have interesting Web sites?

5. What do you do if the information a country provides about itself contradicts information in our textbooks?

6. What skills are necessary before students are capable of reading foreign newspapers?

7. We have libraries full of history books. Why put history on the Web? What information more appropriately belongs in books?

Chapter 9
Curriculum Integration: Humanities

 OVERVIEW

One of the chief beneficiaries of telecommunication capability will be writing classes as students find more audiences to write to and more reasons to write. But extensive resources are also available in the areas of foreign language instruction and the arts.

ENGLISH

While it might seem that English classes would be the last to move into telecommunications, many English teachers have taken the lead in bringing their schools online. Why? There are many applications in the English classroom. A 1995 edition of *The English Journal*, a publication of the National Council of Teachers of English, dedicated an entire issue to the Electronic Classroom. They had ten high school teachers describe the uses they were making of the Internet for writing instruction. Here is an encapsulated description of several of these articles. As you will see, the range of uses is very wide.

"Reading and Writing in a Virtual School," by Harry Noden

Noden began with email by using a PBS bulletin board called Learning Link. His eighth grade students were instructed to email their compositions to the bulletin board where students in other schools around the country read the essays and commented on them. Readers were advised to use PQP (praise, question, polish) as a commenting strategy so students received positive comments along with reminders to correct spelling errors.

"The I-Search Paper Goes Global," by Chris Davis

To help his high school sophomores find more information for research papers, Davis helped his students find a newsgroup on the Internet that was related to each of their research topics. One student was able to use this approach to receive comparisons of various colleges, and another student was able to enliven his report on aliens with lots of first hand reports from people who were absolutely convinced they had been visited from outer space. The real advantage of these newsgroups may be an awareness by students that there are people out there who are currently discussing any topic they could possibly think of. Whether the topic is alien visitors or the works of Thomas Pynchon, there are ongoing electronic discussions involving thousands of people.

"Using Telecomputing Technology to Make World Connections," by Donna Graves

Her eighth grade students sent their essays to a service from America Online called "World Classroom." Her students were free to exchange writing with classrooms around the world that seemed to have similar interests. Several of her students had a lively exchange with some Russian students about Russian music, but the topic quickly turned to current events when President Boris Yeltsin opened fire on his Parliament Building. Students in Moscow gave her students daily eyewitness accounts of the action.

"Canada's Wired Writers," by Trevor Owen

Canada has established a Writer in Electronic Residence (WIER) Program that assigns professional writers to groups of classrooms around the country. Students send their writing to the professional writer and to other schools. They receive reactions both from peers and from the professionals. It gives students an opportunity to learn what professional writers might think of their poetry. For the local teacher, it is a chance to bring additional expertise into the classroom, while the professional can "meet" with students without having to travel around Canada.

"Using Computers to Teach Shakespeare," by Michael LoMonico

LoMonico brings CD-ROM versions of Shakespeare's plays into his classroom. One of his assignments is to have students do word searches. In one assignment, students have a program called "Wordcruncher" count the occurrences of words in "A Midsummer Night's Dream." One girl found the word "take" occurs 24 times, but it is only used twice by females. Her conclusion? Shakespeare's women are passive.

All these teachers have made electronic connections that give their students more practice in writing and reading.

Electronic Resources

What else is available? Quite a few resources and projects have been developed to help English teachers. Here are some of the most important:

Newsday

This is another project of Global Schoolnet. Ten to thirty five classrooms are linked with each of them gathering local news and sending it to the other schools. When enough news stories have been circulated, each school creates its own newspaper. These newspapers are then mailed to the other schools in the project. This gives your students a chance to see what other schools did with the same stories. For more information, contact:

newshelp@gsn.org

National Council of Teachers of English
http://www.ncte.org

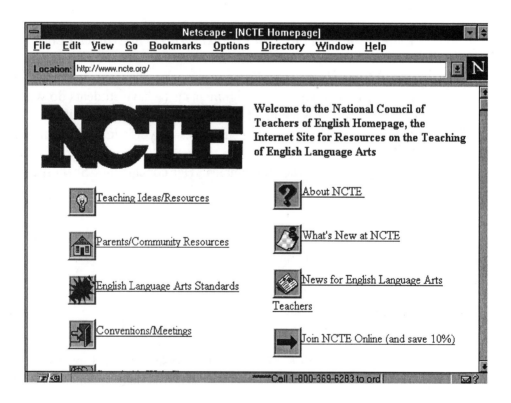

This page leads to many others for the various work groups for NCTE, catalogs for their books, and the current copy of the national standards for English. It also has a large collection of teaching ideas and materials. One committee of NCTE, the Information Literacy Committee, maintains its own Web page with resources and project ideas for teachers who wish to teach information concepts. The address of this page is:

http://www.uwsp.edu/acad/math/infolit2.html

Writer's Resources
http://www.interlog.com/~chi/www/writesource.html

This site serves as a clearinghouse for projects that publish student writing.

Purdue University On-line Writing Lab
http://owl.trc.purdue.edu/prose.html

This site contains many resources for teaching writing, including exercises for students.

Elements of Style
http://www.cc.columbia.edu:80/cis/barttleby/strunk/style.html

A complete grammar handbook on-line.

Shakespeare
http://www.shakespeare.com

This site includes the complete works of Shakespeare with a search tool that will let you find particular words or phrases (who said "hoisted on my own petards"?). It also has updates on all the

Shakespeare festivals scheduled around the world each year, links to discussion groups, and links to recent articles.

FOREIGN LANGUAGES

One of the more interesting listings on the Internet is the number of foreign teachers who are looking for American classrooms to pair up with. Why do they want to link with Americans? They want to give their students a chance to practice written English. Of course the phone lines run in both directions and many American teachers have discovered that they can also use the Internet as a way to give their students practice in French, Spanish, and German.

There are limits, of course. The standard American keyboard doesn't have characters for foreign languages so some adaptations have to be made. For major western languages these adaptations already exist. For eastern languages like Chinese or Japanese, adaptations are still in the works and may take years.

Where are the links? Here are two addresses to start. Each will help you make international connections.

- Intercultural Encounters, St. Olaf College, Northfield, Minnesota
  iecc-request@stolaf.edu

- Kidsphere, Pittsburgh University
  kidsphere@vms.cis.pitt.edu

Foreign Language Materials

Besides giving students access to people of foreign nations, you can also give them access to a wide range of original materials. For instance, Mary Nell Reif, of Wausau, Wisconsin, has created a list of Web sites that she gives to her fourth year Spanish students. Where does she have them go? Foreign language newspapers are a starting place for her.

ABC: A daily newspaper of Spain
http://www.abc.es/htbin/acc-abce

News summaries are printed the same day the originals are published in Spain, so her students can see what the people of Spain are hearing about international events. They can also keep up with major events in Spain. She says the vocabulary is challenging, but worth the effort. She finds that students are excited to be reading "real" Spanish.

Her second favorite site is a collection of links to Spanish sites all over the world. Included are Spanish-language magazines and newspapers, collections of literature, cultural information, tourist information, even comics. Here is the address:

http://www.DocuWeb.ca/SiSpain/sp-home.html

Obviously the same approaches that work for Spanish teachers will work for teachers of any of the major languages. They now have a way of linking their students to children across the globe via email, and of linking them to newspapers and other native-language resources. The result is that students studying a foreign language should have more materials to use, and a greater sense of the communication value of foreign languages.

THE ARTS

It would be nice if we could give our art students weekly tours of the world's major museums. For that matter, even a one-time visit to the Musee D'Orsay is pretty remarkable. Can we begin to make electronic substitutions for these treks? Well, there is no electronic equivalent to being there. And moving large image files across the Internet is still far more complicated (and slow) than moving words. However, there are a growing number of opportunities to access some of the world's fine art.

Where can you find this art?   A good place to start is with the Texas Educational Network (TENET).   TENET is a good site to know about for many reasons. This network provides the teachers of Texas with access to one of the most advanced network resources in the country. Fortunately for teachers elsewhere in the world, Texas is very willing to let outsiders access their Web servers. Here is the first screen of the TENET network with its Web address:

http://www.tenet.edu/depot/main.html

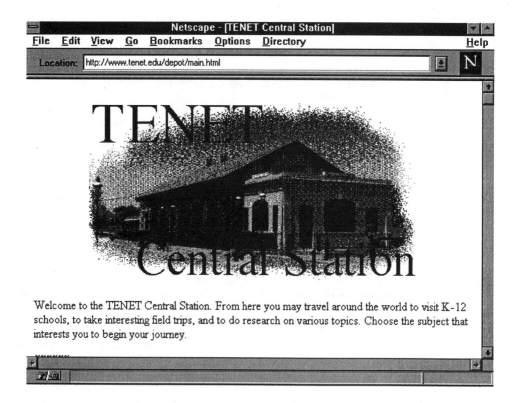

Welcome to the TENET Central Station. From here you may travel around the world to visit K-12 schools, to take interesting field trips, and to do research on various topics. Choose the subject that interests you to begin your journey.

Among the many resources available from TENET at this "Central Station," is a long list of both art and natural history museums. Here are their art museums:

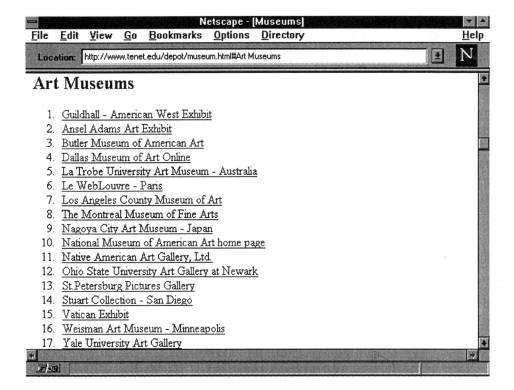

Students can then tour any of the selected museums and download images of their choice. Here is one such example, an Ansel Adams exhibit sponsored by the University of California:

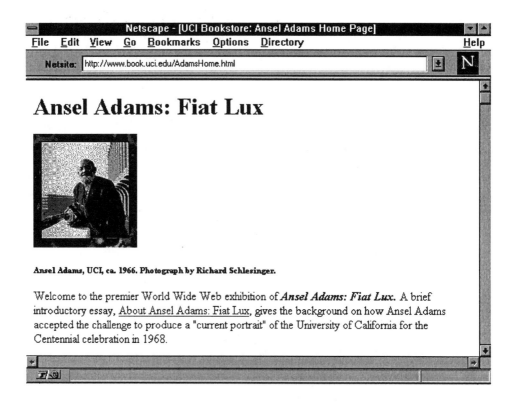

One note of caution. Images are large collections of bits when sent over the Internet, and can take a fairly long time to arrive. The current shortcut in these situations is to have two sizes of Web pictures--small, for you to preview, and large, when you are really sure you want to see the entire image in complete detail. Check the speed of your modem before you venture too far into image capturing. This may be far more time-consuming than you care to try until your equipment is upgraded.

PROJECT SUGGESTIONS

⌐🖰 Sharing essays and stories electronically can be a great experience for students, but it requires that students first get used to responding to the writing of their peers. What process would you use to make students better readers? How might you start them in your own classroom or in small groups so they learn to be helpful critics? A unit plan that took students from local responses to electronic responses would position students to take full advantage of these new media.

⌐🖰 Global Schoolnet and American Online both provide a number of possible links for your students. Use one or the other to connect to schools elsewhere in the world. Find a focus for your discussions.   Over the course of two months you should be able to have your students write two or three assignments and share them with an international audience. Have students make note of messages that surprise them. What do they find out about foreign students that they didn't expect? How do foreign students react to your students' writing?

⌐🖰 Dial up the Web page of a foreign language newspaper. Have your first year students look at the day's news. How much of it can they already understand? Which words do they know or think they know? They should be able to guess much from context and from their own knowledge of current events.

⌐🖰 Make a list of museums you would like your students to see on the World Wide Web. Write a guide for your students. Where should they go? What should they see? What would you have them do at the places they visit?

🐁   If your school has a World Wide Web home page, see if you can add student artwork to it. Many grade schools are already doing this. All it takes is a scanner to digitize art work. You and art teachers around your area could link to each other's pages so students could see the work of their peers.

🖥 DISCUSSION QUESTIONS

1. Connect to NCTE's home page and review their online resources. Which projects seem most attractive to you? What electronic resources would each require (connect-time, World Wide Web capability, etc)?

2. What suggestions do you have about sharing writing electronically? Are there dos and don'ts for students? Most writing teachers already have simple peer review handouts for their students. What changes are required in such handouts for electronic review?

3. How much time does this take? By the time students do some writing and send it out electronically, is it days, weeks?

4. What are good topics for international writing exchanges?

5. Do you have experience with team teaching where an English teacher and a social studies teacher team up to work on a common international assignment? List three or four project ideas that seem especially appropriate for such team-teaching.

6. What are some hot sites for foreign language exchanges?

7. What are some hot sites for art exchanges?

RECOMMENDED READING

Davis, C. The I-Search Paper Goes Global: Using the Internet as a Research Tool. *English Journal*, October 1995, 84:27-33.

Graves, D. Using Telecomputing Technology to Make World Connections in the Writing Class. *English Journal*, October 1995, 84:41-44.

LoMonico, M. Using Computer to Teach Shakespeare. *English Journal*, October 1995, 84:58-61.

Noden, H. A Journey through Cyberspace: Reading and Writing in a Virtual School. *English Journal*, October 1995, 84:19-26.

Owen, T. Poems that Change the World: Canada's Wired Writers. *English Journal*, October 1995, 84:48-52.

Rice, C. G. Bring Intercultural Encounters in Classrooms: IECC Electronic Mailing Lists. *THE Journal*, January 1996, 60-63.

Chapter 10
The School Library:
Books in a Digital World

 **OVERVIEW**

What does the information highway mean for librarians? Studies show school librarians are usually the most knowledgeable about these issues and the first to put digital links into their offices. But how do they merge the old and the new? What is the place for books?

EMERGING INFORMATION RESOURCES

CD-ROMs

While much of our attention has been focused on distant resources, an important alternative is the CD-ROM. The attractiveness of the CD is its capacity--640 million bytes. If "bytes" don't work for you as a frame of reference, another way of explaining the capacity of a CD is 300,000 typed pages. That would be a stack three stories high. In other words, one little CD disk can hold several hundred books or several thousand magazines. For libraries cramped for space, the CD is a divine invention.

The other advantage of CDs is the fact that text on them is stored digitally. This means computers can search through the text just as they would look through programs on a floppy disk. So computers can do searches for articles, look through text for key words, and pull out passages that students might want to use in their research papers. In short, text on a CD is more convenient than text on paper.

While it might seem that CDs are a form of competition to on-line resources, they are actually just another form of digital text. For a student doing a subject search, the interfaces she sees and the actions she takes to get to an article don't really differ much whether the article she wants is on a CD in her own computer, on a CD sitting on a network server, or on a Web site sitting in Tokyo. The information is in digital form, it is sitting on some storage device, and it will be loaded into her computer if she asks for it.

For that reason, most librarians simply consider CDs one of a mix of resources. They take up little space, supply a huge number of articles the library may not have had before, and can give students cheap experience in doing on-line searches. Are they a good replacement for books? No. Are they a good replacement for magazines? Yes. They take up less space, are easier to search, and don't waste space with ads.

On-line Databases

While CDs are relatively cheap since the library has to pay for them only once and then has unlimited use, CDs go out of date. They often need to be replaced quarterly. An alternative is to go on-line to one of the commercial databases like Dialog. These databases contain huge amounts of information, far more than even a collection of CDs, and the databases are constantly updated by professionals.

The disadvantage of on-line databases are the need to dial up the database (so a phone line and modem is tied up), the need to pay subscription and connection fees, and the fact that the databases are so large they seem cumbersome for children to use. Most libraries have the librarian do the actual search, which means the librarian is burdened with hours of searching.

University Card Catalogs

An increasingly common activity for high school libraries is to dial up the local university and let students search their on-line catalog. The point is to give college-bound students some experience with a skill that will be essential to them when they go to college. It is also often an eye-opener for students who may have no idea at all how much has been published on any conceivable subject. Most university libraries already have dial-in facilities for their own off-campus students, so the resources are already there for high schools.

The requirements for this activity are a phone line and a modem and some patience. There is still no standard interface for university systems, so students may find rather odd screen displays and arcane commands.

On-line Libraries

With the popularization of the World Wide Web, a number of organizations are creating on-line libraries. One is "Electric Library" (Figure 10-1).

Users can do a subject search and retrieve complete texts of books, magazine articles, or transcripts of radio and television programs relevant to the subject. This particular electronic library has thousands of sources, but it doesn't have all of them. Many of the major magazines are not included. It should also be pointed out that this is a commercial site with a subscription fee. For more information, including costs, use their address:

http://www.elibrary.com

Figure 10-1

A different approach is being taken by a group of students at the University of Michigan. They have created the Internet Public Library which has a large variety of services on-line, from book recommendations to Ask the Author to reference services. Figure 10-2 shows what their home page looks like.

This is an interesting experiment, but it is still just an experiment, with no permanent funding base yet. It does give a sense, however, of what librarians might be able to do in the future.

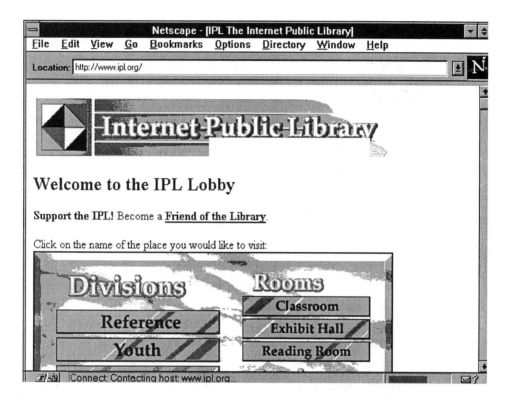

Figure 10-2

Sources for Librarians

While there is a great deal available on-line for library users, there are also a number of important resources for librarians themselves. Here are a few lead resources:

LM_NET
This is a discussion group for library media specialists. Send the usual subscription message to **listserv@suvm.syr.edu**

CDROM-L
This is a discussion group on CD-ROMs. Send a subscription message to **listserv@uccvma.ucop.edu**

Banned Books
http://www-cgi.cs.cmu.edu/Web/People/spok/banned-books.html
This Web page describes books being banned in American schools.

BUDGETING

What does all of this cost? This is not a time when schools have extra dollars. How can a library keep buying books when it also needs to be putting in phone lines and buying CDs and budgeting for on-line access fees? The truth is few libraries can afford the extra costs.

One solution has been to cut other places in the budget. If we are getting articles on CD-ROM, can we cut back on periodical purchases? Yes, at least to some extent. Journals are very costly and they take up lots of space. Having fewer around is a blessing for most librarians.

Can we buy fewer books? Maybe. There is no real substitute for great books. They are easy to carry around, take up little space, and can be accessed (read) by hundreds of students over the years. Books have a place in every library. But are all books necessary? Some books that summarize current events have a shelf-life of just a year or two. The information they present can be covered more cheaply and more properly by articles available on CDs. Librarians nationwide are looking at books and asking "Is this one going to be useful for more than a year or two?"

But even with substantial cuts in periodical purchases and small cuts in book purchases, not nearly enough is saved to cover the costs of the new materials needed by a library. Now they need computers, networks, phone lines, CDs, access fees, and phone charges. These are all new costs. Where is that money coming from? Usually from additional budget requests. Libraries are becoming more expensive.

WIRING

As library budgets weren't already being pushed past their limits, we are about to see a new level of demand. Currently school libraries maintain most of their resources locally. CD-ROMs facilitate the maintenance of this situation. Where libraries have phone access, it tends to be a single line that gives the librarian email access, or lets students dial up a university card catalog, or lets a librarian reach a major on-line database like Dialog. One line may not be ideal, but it can handle much of the demand.

Two new demands are pushing libraries to go with more phone lines. One demand is sharing between libraries. If a district has multiple schools, it would be nice if teachers at any school could find out what books are available anywhere in the district. They can, but only if all school libraries are on-line. Then the district has to set up a wide area network (WAN) to link all the schools. Once those schools are linked, why not link with neighboring districts, or with the community library? Districts are doing just that, but all of this requires more lines between libraries.

The World Wide Web creates another demand for lines. Not only does it provide a huge set of important resources that can only be accessed on-line, but many of those resources are graphic, meaning they are large files that require fast phone lines for quick transfer. Having one World Wide Web station in the library won't be enough--once teachers see what's on the Web, there is too much demand for it. But each line, whether it is two, or five, or ten, will meet only part of the demand and, of course, add major costs for installation and upkeep. If there is a financial black hole for libraries, the Web might be it.

TRAINING

As we bring new resources into our libraries, we need to teach students how to use these new materials. There are many approaches that librarians are taking.

Here are three that seem the most common:

Early Start. Just as students are learning keyboarding skills in grades four through six, many schools are building in library skill units at roughly the same age. Classes of young students are brought to the library to do mock searches. The librarian demonstrates each of the CD-ROM computers and shows students how to enter a key word for basic searching. The advantage of this approach is that students are now ready to use the new tools. The disadvantage is that some of them may not be called upon to do any research for years and will forget (or the library will have changed by the time they actually do a search).

Lead Assignment. This is a cooperative approach in which some middle school teacher decides to take the lead and give students their first larger research paper assignment. The teacher helps identify research topics and describes the intent of the paper. Then the librarian steps in and provides much of the technical instruction in how to use the tools of the library. Once students have been through this initial assignment, they have the skills they need to do similar research in other classes.

Search Assistant.   Even at the high school level, you often find librarians who hide part of the research task from students. This often occurs with on-line database searches where students will be responsible to determine a subject, but a library aide will do the actual computer work, accessing the on-line database and typing in the search keys. This approach may be necessary where databases are complicated and difficult to understand, but of course it not only places a severe practical limit on the librarians, but it also leaves students no better informed about how to do searches than when they started the assignment.

A TYPICAL ASSIGNMENT

Helen Adams, Library Director of the Rosholt, Wisconsin Public Schools has developed a high school library with a mix of all the resources listed above, plus a range of the traditional materials--books, magazines, and encyclopedias. Given that environment, it is common for teachers in the school to expect their students to do multiple searches. Students are expected to look for local books in the card catalog and university books in the UW-Stevens Point on-line card catalog. They are also to use on-line encyclopedias and printed encyclopedias and several different CD-ROM article collections.

Library staff will help with searches and will provide training for students in general library skills, but students are expected to do most of their own work. They cannot settle for one information source like books, for example, but must use all the avenues. To prove that they have actually checked through the CD-ROM article collections, they are asked to print out a paper or two showing their search results. This evidence is attached to the end of their research paper.

As a result, it is clear that students are being expected to learn two things simultaneously. First, of course, they are learning about the subject they are researching. Given these new information channels they are getting more data and more timely information than they could have before. So they are learning in their content area. But it is clear there is a second agenda in all these assignments. Students are being taught general information skills. Specifically, they are being taught:

- Information now exists in digital form.
- It is stored in a range of formats.
- It can be searched for with multiple tools.
- Connections exist to "reach" for information anywhere in the world.

Clearly all of these are basic skills for the information age.

PROJECT SUGGESTIONS

🖱 Each library should be establishing a migration plan to get from current resources to the resources it wants to have. A great project would be to gather a committee and work out such a plan. It should include not only descriptions of resources, but plans for budgeting, training, wiring, and selling the school board and community on the project.

🖱 Another good project would involve a research project for students. It would include an assignment, a teaching plan for instructing them on the use of current library resources, grading strategies, and cooperative plans with library personnel. In short, what would a research assignment that did an effective job of helping students learn about the modern library look like?

🖳 DISCUSSION QUESTIONS

1. What are the best CDs? If you had to name the top ten for any school library, what would you include?

2. Which are the best and worst on-line databases? What is the future of commercial databases, given the rapid growth of Gopher and the World Wide Web?

3. What is your school spending for CDs and on-line access? Has that mix changed over the last three years?

4. What magazines have you stopped purchasing in the last several years? Have you cut back on books?

5. Describe an assignment that helps students learn library skills. Be sure to fully describe the role of the classroom teacher and the role of the school librarian.

Chapter 11

Training and Professional Resources for Teachers

 ## OVERVIEW

Most of our interest in the Internet is how it will benefit our students. But we also have our own needs. What resources are there that we can use professionally? It turns out there are many professional resources being placed on the Net. The other question for teachers is how are they to learn about these resources? Are there helpful training models for teacher educators?

RESOURCES FOR TEACHERS

Email

When the state of Texas began creating the Texas Educational Network, it began with the premise that a computer linked to TENET would sit on the desk of every teacher in the state. The network would be first and foremost a teacher's resource. An essential part of that resource would be nothing more complicated than simple electronic mail. Their sense was that teachers, even more than students, need email.

Why email? If you think about it, teachers are virtually inaccessible during the work day. They can call out at lunch (if they don't have lunchroom duty), or during a prep period (if they actually get one), but are totally tied up the rest of the day. Enter email. Like voice mail, you can leave a message even if the person is busy or out of the room. Unlike voice mail, you can leave a message even if the phone lines are busy--the network will keep retrying until it can pass the message on. The value of this avenue of communication is best demonstrated by two teachers at Rosholt High School. They teach in the same hallways of the same building. Yet they never get a chance to talk during the day. Their solution? They send email messages to each other before and after school.

Local Lists

If getting a hold of one teacher seems difficult, imagine trying to speak with a group, all at different schools. Yet that is the situation faced weekly by district athletic directors. The solution? Athletic directors in Wisconsin are in the process of forming their own electronic mail connection so they can exchange scores from local competitions and information about their teams. One of the most critical times for these directors is tournament time when football teams may be playing games all over the state. Each team wants to know the outcome of games elsewhere in the state so they know who they will play next. Email will give them that information faster and with fewer phone calls.

Professional Lists

Discussion lists are so convenient as a communications avenue that there are thousands of them. How are teachers to find out about all the lists that are available in each interest area? Fortunately, there are indexes to these lists. One such index is found in Figure 11-1. The address for this particular index is:

http://www.tile.net/tile/listserv/index.html

Figure 11-1

You can search for a specific topic, or browse using the listings provided. You will be surprised by the large number of lists available for teachers. To get a sense of just how many lists are available, here are some Special Education lists and their addresses. Clearly, there are many discussion groups available for educators.

Special Education

ADA-LAW   Americans with Disabilities Act Law discussion
                 @ndsuvm1

ALTLEARN   Alternative approaches to learning
                 @sjuvm

ASLING-L   American Sign Language list
                 @yalevm

AUTISM   SJU autism and developmental disabilities
                 @sjuvm

AXSLIB-L   Issues of disabled access to libraries
                 @rbanks@uwstout

BEHAVIOR   Behavioral & emotional disorders in children
                 @asuacad

BLIND-L   Computer use by and for the blind
                 @uafsysb

BLINDNWS   Blind News Digest
                 @ndsuvm1

BRAILLE   Discussion list for blind in Czech. & England
                 @searn

CDMAJOR   Communication Disorder discussion list
                 @kentvm

CHATBACK   Planning forum for Chatback UK & Int'l;
                 educational net for disabled children
                 @sjuvm

COMMDIS   Speech disorders
                 @rpitsvm

DDFIND-L	Forum for networking on disabilities **@gitvm1**
DEAF-L	Deaf list **@siucvmb**
DISRES-L	Disability research list **@ryerson**
DSSHE-L	Disabled Student Services in Higher Ed. admins. disc **@ubvm**
EASILIBXS	Equal Access to Software & Information for disabled email: **easi@um.cc.umich.edu**
ETEXT	Electronic text formatting for the disabled email: **easi@um.cc.umich.edu**
EYEMOV-L	Eye Movement network **@spcvxa**
L-HCAP	Handicapped people in education **@ndsuvm1**
MOBILITY	SJU mobility disabilities list **@sjuvm**
SCR-L	Study of cognitive rehabilitation **@mizzou1**
SPCEDS-L	Special education students list--Suny/Buffalo **@ubvm**
STUT-HLP	Support list for stutterers and their families **@bgu.edu**

| STUTT-L | Stuttering Research & clinical practice **@templevm** |
| TALKBACK | Kids forum for CHATBACK **@sjuvm** |

Finding Discussion Groups for Teachers

It takes almost nothing to start a discussion group, so new ones spring up every day. Some are built around a particular interest or geographical region, others are built around existing professional bodies. A good place to look for discussion groups that would be useful to you is your own professional organizations. For example, the National Council of Teachers of English (NCTE) has two main groups:

NCTE-talk@itc.org
English-Teachers@ux1.cso.uiuc.edu

Most teacher's groups have set up similar discussion groups. Other groups have been set up or coordinated by state departments of education. Texas has its own educational network (TENET) and most states make some effort to help teachers get connected to other teachers. As a result, you should find that many of the places you went to in the past for education information will be the places you can contact now for network information.

In some cases, network providers themselves have created special lists for teachers. America Online, for example, has created its own groups for teachers. They will give you the latest information about such groups when they give you subscriber information.

Joining a Group

Specialized computer programs handle most of the electronic mail for discussion groups. *Listserv* is the program used most often on Internet. It can add you to a list if it knows two things about you--your email address, and your real name. Therefore, the usual process is to find out the address of the program that controls the discussion group. It is usually listserv@[some address]. You send a message to that address saying you want to subscribe to the list. Let's use an example.

NCTE has a group called NCTE-talk. As we saw before, the Internet address of this group is:

NCTE-talk@itc.org

itc.org gives me the address for the group. So to get a message to the program controlling the list, I would send a request to the *listserv* at this address. That address would look like this:

listserv@itc.org

What message do I send? I send only one line:

subscribe NCTE-talk Bill Wresch

I told the controlling program which group I wish to join (NCTE-talk) and then I gave it my name. Within a few hours I should get a message back saying I have been added to the list, and from then on all mail to group members will come to me as well.

How do I get out of a group? I may want to quit a group if I run out of time, find out the group doesn't match my interests, or if I simply find the volume of mail overwhelming. To quit, I just send a message to the same place I used when I first signed up. Only this time I send:

unsubscribe NCTE-talk

What does discussion on a listserv look like? Here is a series of messages that appeared on the listserv of the National Council of Teachers of English. As you will see, they tend to be an interesting mix of the personal and the professional.

On Mon, 27 Nov 1995 HUHS_ST@mail wrote:

> **I have a dozen or so easy to read poems about football**
> **that would interest 9th graders. I don't really want**
> **to kill them by discussing each poem, one at a time,**
> **in a group discussion. But I would like to get more**
> **out of them than just to spend a period reading them.**
>
> **Any suggestions? Thanks in advance.**
>
> **Jean**
>
>

Jean,

You might try breaking your classes into small groups, and giving each group a poem to present to the rest of the class.

OR

You might use the same groups and ask each of them to read one poem and then write a poem about a different subject, imitating the poem (students in the group would write their poems individually)

Sincerely,

Sarah

An earlier responder's suggestions about preparing readers for the elliptical quality of some of Faulkner's writing brought to mind a section of *As I Lay Dying* that would be perfect for this purpose. It's Dewey Dell's recollection of the first time she and Lafe "picked on down the row," which

comes fairly early in the novel. It's a short section -- only a few paragraphs -- and it's self-contained in that it tells a powerful story that stands alone. Having readers make sense of it in small groups and then share their understandings would work well.

Gloria   Lynn Haven, FL

Hi everyone! I finally got some mail. However, the KSU system is still messed up. I typed up a long message an hour ago, but when I tried to send it, the system crashed and I lost it. So, I'll try again, even though I should probably be reading Henry James right now.

First, thanks to Gary, Barbara, and Reinhold for letting me know I wasn't lost in space. I got 53 messages today!

This example illustrates the best and the worst aspects of lists. They can be valuable links to your professional colleagues around the world. But they also seem to be chatty. Some lists are more chatty than others, but any list poses the risk of burying you in email. You will find yourself getting on and off many lists before you find the ones that have the content and style that match your needs and interests.

Index Sites

With so many Web pages now available in every subject, it has become impossible for people to keep up with what is out there. It really can be a full-time job just to surf the Net and identify sites that are available. Fortunately, there are a growing number of index sites that serve as indexes to other Web sites. Each provides a great jumping off place for searches.

In education there are four main sites that you will find of special value. Each provides an index to many interesting educational resources.

Uncle Bob's Kid's Page
http://gagme.wwa.com/~boba/kids.html

Kathy Schrock's Guide to Educators
http://www.capecod.net/Wixon/wixon.htm

Texas Educational Network
http://www.tenet.edu

Jan Wee's Favorite Sites
http://www.state.wi.us/agencies/dpi/www/jan_bkm.html

Most of the sites resemble the one from Jan Wee. They list recommended sites by subject are and have interactive links, so if any resource looks good, you just click on that line and jump to that site.

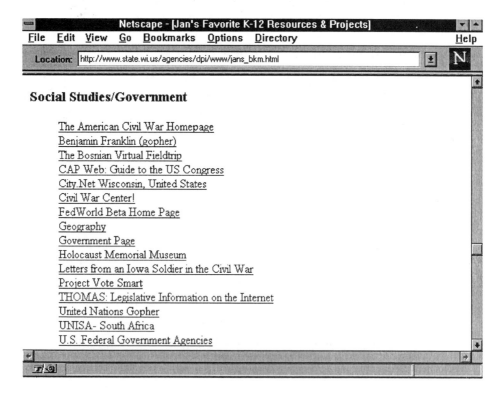

Professional Resources

The Educational Resources Information Center (ERIC) has long been a primary information source for teachers doing research. Usually it took a trip to a university library to access their materials. Now teachers with World Wide Web access can do a search from their classroom. Here is the address of the ERIC web site:

http://ericir.syr.edu/ERIC/eric.html

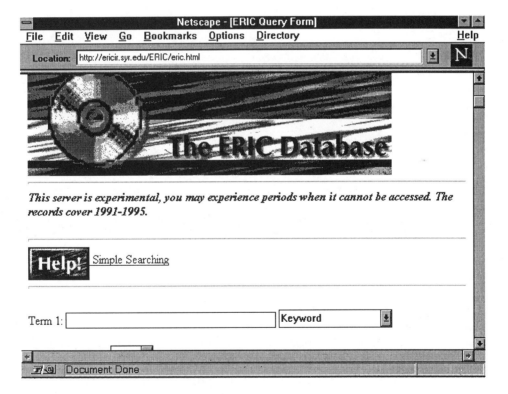

Searching works much as it always has. You type in two or three key words, and let ERIC find the research that has been done on your topic. In the example below, I did a search on "basketball" and "mathematics skills". The search took just over two seconds and brought up the following resources:

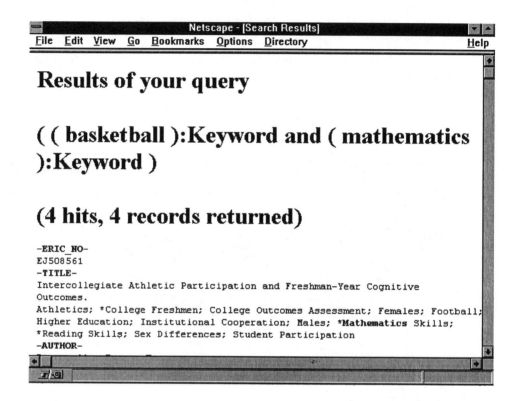

Clearly, teachers with Web access have a very convenient way to do educational research.

One other resource is available through ERIC--lesson plans (Figure 11-2). They maintain a series of links to the growing number of organizations that provide lesson plans to teachers, including NASA and CNN. The address for this service is:

gopher://ericir.syr.edu:70/11/Lesson

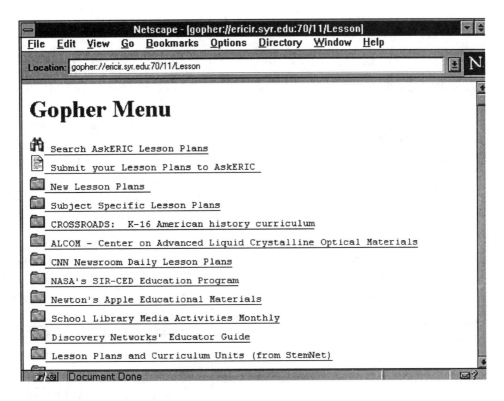

Figure 11-2

TEACHER TRAINING

Terri Iverson does teacher training for CESA #3 in Platteville, Wisconsin. She is convinced that districts put far too little effort into teacher training. They put in the hardware and software, but don't tell teachers enough about how to use the Internet well. The result? The technology sits unused. Good point. But what is a proper training method for teachers? Many approaches have been tried. A recent ERIC publication (Harris, 1995) lists 8 approaches (Table 11-1):

Table 11-1

Method	Description
Independent learning	Time-consuming and frustrating, but it works for some teachers. The problem is getting the time.
Independent learning with remote assistance	Do what you can locally and call for help from network specialists when you need it.
One-to-one coaching	As communities of telecomputing teachers develop, this will become more common.
Large-group demonstration with independent practice	This model is more effective for marshaling support from decision makers than for helping teachers use the Internet.
Large-group demonstration with assisted practice	An improvement over the model above, but not as effective as the next three.
Hands-on bab, Intensive schedule	Built around several half-days or full Saturdays.
Hands-on lab, Paced schedule	Spreads the work evenly over a semester so teachers have time to practice between sessions.
Hands-on, paced, with structured on-line activities	Requires structured, motivating, on-line activities to be performed by teachers between sessions.

The eight approaches above describe a range of techniques. What they don't describe is content. What should teachers be taught? One recent survey conducted of over one hundred teachers in Wisconsin established this list of priorities:

1. Email. The thought here was that teachers would want to know more about telecommunications and would use it more frequently if they were given email accounts and started receiving email.

2. Curriculum materials. The advocates of this approach suggest the first thing to do is get teachers to Web sites in their subject area. Once teachers see all that is available to them, they will put in the effort to learn what they need.

3. Search engines. The point here is twofold. One is to give teachers a means to find what is on the Web. The second is to build a bridge between the familiar, library searching, and the new, the Internet.

4. Hardware. This is the more technical approach. Teachers are given explanations of how telecommunications works, definitions of terms like "modem" and "bandwidth," and lengthy experience with telecommunications software. At first blush this seems exactly the wrong approach since it explains "how" without giving teachers much grounding in "why." It can also turn away the technologically challenged (those of us whose VCR still blinks 12:00). But before rejecting this approach totally, it is worth remembering that Internet connections can be complicated and teachers who don't understand them can become very frustrated when connections just seem to disappear without reason. Teachers who really understand how the process works may be better able to establish links and to troubleshoot the inevitable breakdowns.

5. Professional Uses. This approach begins with the view that Internet resources are so limited in most schools it will be years before we can make them generally available to students. Given this, why not reserve limited Internet resources for teachers? Give teachers a year or two when they can use email to contact peers, do research for graduate courses they might be taking, or just surf the Net out of curiosity. Teachers can gain experience with the system away from the possibility of public embarrassment in front of students, they can learn what the resource can do, and they will be far more ready to use the system with students when the school finally has enough phone lines to open this opportunity to children. The only disadvantage to this approach is that until students come home from school bragging about all the great things they are doing on the Internet, there may never be the public push for more phone lines.

PROJECT SUGGESTIONS

Sign on to a listserv discussion group for at least several weeks. Keep a log of the number of messages each day. Can you categorize the kind of questions that are asked? What was the quality of the answers? How would you describe the nature of the electronic conversations: Professional? Casual? Personal? Ask a question or make a comment on the listserv. What kind of reaction do you get? What did you expect?

If you were going to do a series of workshops for teachers in your school, how would you organize the inservices? What materials would you give out? How much hands-on work would you do? How would you schedule your time? How would you determine the effectiveness of your workshops?

DISCUSSION QUESTIONS

1. Teachers frequently have better email access at home than they do at school. Are the biggest barriers to email access at school technical, or policy matters?

2. What are good discussion lists that you would recommend? How did you find out about the lists?

3. If you created a Web page with your favorite sites, which would you recommend?

4. Have you used the ERIC system over the Internet? Do you have recommendations for its use?

5. If you were going to train the other teachers in your school about the Internet, what topics would you include? What activities would you include?

RECOMMENDED READING

Harris, J. (1995) Teaching Teachers to Use Telecommunications Tools. Rockville, MD: Educational Resources Information Center. [This is a **free** booklet. Dial 1-800-LET-ERIC for a copy.]

Chapter 12
District Planning, Wiring, and Acceptable Use

 ## OVERVIEW

While classroom teachers will take the lead in using the information highway, there are a variety of technical and budgetary issues that require the joint involvement of teachers and administrators. This chapter reviews some of the decisions they have to make, and provides some guidance for them.

A DISTRICT VISION

In visiting school districts that were leading in the use of telecommunications, it was universally the case that the administrators could tell me instantly why the Internet was important to students and to the community. They didn't need to think about it and didn't need to rehearse before they went on camera. They could explain clearly and succinctly why the district was doing what it was doing. It was clear they had given this talk many times before, to PTOs, Lion's Clubs, and up and down Main Street.

It seems to me that if districts are going to be effective, they need to follow the lead of William Andrekopoulos, Dean Isaacson, Kathleen Martinson, and Erwin Roth and begin with a vision. What are we trying to do here, and why is it important to this community? This has to be a shared vision, one grounded in the particular needs of the local schools. But there are common reasons we see for all schools to use the Internet:

- It leads to jobs.
- It will help us connect to the world.
- It will help the world find out about us.
- It will strengthen _____ part of the curriculum.
- Students going on to college will need it.
- Students will need it in the workplace.
- Schools need to keep up with what some students have in their homes.

Whatever the reasons for moving to use of the Internet, they have to resonate in the local community. How do districts find that vision? Most begin with conversations among technology experts, teachers, administrators, and community leaders--which is another way of saying they begin with a planning process.

PLANNING PROCESS

The Rosholt, Wisconsin School District has one model for planning that may be useful to other districts. It began with important decisions about who should do the planning. The assumption they made was that planning really has two purposes. The first is to arrive at valid decisions about what action should be taken. But the second, and equally important purpose, is to communicate (sell) the plan to all the stakeholders in the school.

So, who they did put on the planning committee? Helen Adams was their technology expert. She had been wiring her library for years and was actively involved with teachers in classroom technology projects. She knew what was out there, and what teachers were doing with it. This is an important combination of skills. To ensure that teachers were heard, there were several of them from a range of grade levels. To ensure that the project had administrative support, there was an administrator from each level--grade school, middle school, and high school. To ensure that there was community support and input, they brought in a school board member, Dave Eschenbach, who participated in all the committee meetings, and then helped keep the rest of the board informed of directions the committee was taking.

Such a committee seems ideal. It brings a range of voices to the room so there is less likelihood of the committee running off in odd directions. It ensures that all groups within the district are heard. No group feels left out. It ensures that the committee will have powerful representatives when the time comes to act on the plan. Those who have budget authority are in the room and know what will be needed and why the money has to be found.

What do committees like these do over the course of their one to two year lifetime? Each takes some or all of the following steps:

Review current situation. What technology is already in the district? What do teachers know? What activities are already occurring in classrooms? What infrastructure exists?

Review current possibilities. What are other districts already doing? Many committees will send representatives to other schools or to state conferences.

Predict future. Where is the technology heading? What resources are coming on line? Beside reading relevant journals, committees often invite phone company or computer company representatives in to describe directions they are moving with their products.

Build a timeline. What can be done over each of the next five years? Who will do it? Actions each year may appear modest, but they eventually accumulate.

Build a budget. This needs to include costs for technology, teacher training, and support personnel.

Check back with constituencies. Does the first draft of the plan include all that it needs to include? Is it headed in a direction that gathers support from the community? Is it likely to be accepted as a blueprint for the district?

Revise the plan. The committee needs to realize some of their best ideas simply won't sell, and that some really good ideas can come from people who aren't on the committee. Here is their chance to demonstrate flexibility.

Sell the plan. Once the plan has been revised, do all members of the committee understand they have a responsibility to make the plan work? They were selected for their brilliance and for their persuasive powers. Now it is time to use those persuasive powers.

Implement and update. Who will ensure that the plan is more than just 50 pages of paper sitting in a filing cabinet? Who will give regular reports on actions taken and actions needed?

All districts have experience with planning committees. Some of those experiences are good; some are pretty awful. Careful selection of the committee, and careful planning of committee time can at least help the process go in the right direction.

WIRING

While this is one of the areas we usually leave to the professionals, there are several aspects of wiring that teachers using computers should at least know about in general terms.

Electricity

Computers and network routers (which are really computers dedicated to network traffic) pose problems for electrical circuits. They need a steady level of power free of surges, spikes, and brownouts. Yet our school buildings, especially older buildings, are often underwired and overused. We hang a variety of appliances on our electrical grids that no one anticipated in 1922. The result may be that even though our classrooms have a variety of outlets in them, the power coming from the outlets may not be good enough. Somebody needs to check--often over a period of hours--to see if the electrical outlets will do what you need them to do. Without taking this precaution, you may be looking at significant computer maintenance bills down the road.

Phone Lines

For the first teacher or two in a building who wants to use the Internet, it may be relatively simple to run an extra line into the building and down to the library or classroom. But what happens for the next teachers? Do you want to run individual lines into each room gradually as they are needed, or would it be better to wire phone jacks into all rooms at once? Do you want to treat each line as a separate entity, just like another line to your home, or do you want to route all of them to a building switch--a Private Branch Exchange (PBX)? This is the time to get a phone company rep in to show cost comparisons for each approach.

Local Area Network

Do you want to connect each computer directly to a phone line, or do you want to connect a group of computers to a local area network (LAN)? That local area network can share resources like CD-ROM drives, local email, and networked software. It can also have a modem attached so that you can connect to the Internet through it. Now you have access to the Internet from any machine on the LAN, but remember that only one machine at a time can call out, since you still have only one phone line. The exception would be if you have a direct connect (leased line) from the LAN to some Internet service provider (ISP). Now, if you pay for enough bandwidth, multiple computers can access the Internet at the same time. But of course you need to pay for that level of capacity.

Wide Area Network

School libraries usually take the lead here. They want to link all the libraries in the district. Next some building principal will decide it is a good idea to be able to send email back to the district office. Soon all the buildings are being wired together in a Wide Area Network (WAN). This effort takes careful planning. Will each building send all its traffic to a single point on the WAN, or will there be multiple access points for each LAN? How will traffic be controlled? How will different computer systems be integrated? (The district office may have a large computer system from IBM, while the schools may have collections of microcomputers from Apple and other vendors.) Organizing the interaction of all these computers is called network "topology," and is handled by specialists. But teachers should be aware that any WAN requires extra work and usually involves compromises over network service. On the other hand, it is one way to get more access across the district.

COSTS

Costs start simply--one teacher, one phone line, twenty to forty dollars a month, more if long distance charges are involved or if children are on-line for many hours. But at least at the outset, costs seem within the realm of reason. Illinois Senator Everett Dirkson was famous for saying about government spending, "A billion here, a billion there, pretty soon it begins to add up." For school districts, it is the twenty dollar connect fees that begin to add up.

Russell Rothstein was a visiting researcher at the US Department of Education in 1994 when they asked him to do a cost analysis of telecommunications for school districts. He then expanded his work while at MIT in 1995. His numbers are scary to say the least. He begins with four models for implementation.

Model 1   A single PC with dial up connection to the Internet. Rough costs--$5 per student per year.

Model 2   A local area network in the school with a modem connection to the Internet. Rough costs--$30 per student per year.

Model 3   Local area network with a router linking the LAN to the Internet. Rough costs--$30 per student per year.

Model 4   A local area network with a dedicated line to the Internet. Rough costs--$40 per student per year.

Rothstein also provides some breakdown of where schools will incur their costs. He makes it clear phone costs and technology purchases are only half of total district costs. Teacher training and system support are fully half of the expenses. Here are his figures:

telecommunications	11%
retrofitting	7%
hardware	36%
training	13%
support	33%

As one consequence of this cost mix, Rothstein points out that even if phone companies gave away connect time for free, costs for districts would still be substantial. Much of the money is going for hardware and for people.

GENERATING PUBLIC SUPPORT

These additional costs for telecommunications underscore the need to garner public support for this venture. Without the help of parents and voters, it will be very difficult to add Internet activities to our curricula. How can we gain that support? Here are four approaches that have been used successfully in Wisconsin:

1. Involve the public in planning. We have already described the success the Rosholt District has had by doing what really should be obvious--involving taxpayers in decisions about their money.

2. Train parents. Newspapers currently seem indifferent or negative to the Internet. They often portray it as a place for wackos and criminals. The best way to show parents why there is a real need for their children to get on the Net is to put parents on the Net. Districts that hold classes for parents on the Internet are finding that classes are filled instantly. Each of these parents can then converse at the coffee shop the next morning on where they went on the net and what they learned.

3. Work with local businesses. An amazing number of small businesses are setting up sites for themselves on the World Wide Web and selling products on-line. As you find out about local businesses that take this step, be sure to pass that information along to administrators and to parents. Have students surf over to the local site. They too will be impressed that local folks are taking the plunge.

4. Include Internet activities in open house materials. Make sure students print some of the letters they are getting from overseas. Describe how you are using the connection in classes. Parents need to see that the Internet is not some trendy new activity, but a new avenue to learn the old reliable skills--the basics.

ACCEPTABLE USE

Pornography

In January 1996, the German government charged CompuServe's German operation with allowing pornographic materials to circulate on the local net.

They wanted it stopped. There are two issues at play here: free speech and commercial responsibility. In the case of free speech, we have the traditional problem of when erotic materials cross the line and become pornographic. This is a difficult line to define and is often left to local values. Since the Internet is international, we may now be faced with the novel situation of one judge in Bavaria deciding the matter for the entire planet. The second issue for CompuServe was whether they had any responsibility for the messages traveling across their system. The argument they made is that they are just like mail carriers--they just move messages without reading them. If the post office can't be sued for sending pornographic materials, how can CompuServe be sued? They are not like television that sells a product and therefore has some responsibility for what that product looks like.

While these arguments will be the focus of intense political and legal debate, there are two things certain at the moment. The first is that CompuServe agreed to shut down several sites that carried pornographic material. CompuServe gave in. The second certainty is that there is material on the Net that people find objectionable. Some material is shocking to adults, and certainly is not something we would like to see in the hands of children. How much of this material is there? Pick your survey. One study frequently cited by religious fundamentalists implies most of the Net is carrying pornography. This is the famous Carnegie-Mellon study. The problem with the study is that it was done by a graduate student, is apparently very flawed, and was never approved by Carnegie Mellon University--he just happened to be a student there. Other studies indicate the problem is far smaller, a minuscule slice of Internet traffic.

As teachers, we need to be aware of the real problem so we don't overreact or underreact, but we also need to have policies and procedures in place that will ensure our students use the Internet for educational purposes. More on that later.

Harassment

People send some very strange things over email. At a community college in Northern California teachers set up two email lists, one for male students and one for females. Soon talk got pretty wild. Before the semester was over lots of ugly things were being mailed back and forth. Two of the women in the class saw what was being said about them on the men's mail list and went for their lawyers. The college ended up paying the women thousands of dollars, and the email list disappeared.

In a famous case at the University of Michigan, a young man sent a short story over the Net in which he described a number of violent things he wanted to do to his ex-girl friend. He claimed it was just a story, she claimed it was a threat, and the lawyers joined in.

here is a common problem on computer networks called "flaming." People who seem nice enough person to person, seem to lose all inhibitions and say lots of ugly things via email. We can leave the reasons for this to psychologists. As teachers, he position we face is that students can say things to other students (or their teachers) that simply aren't permissible. Rules of speech have to be established and enforced.

Hate Speech

Do the rights of free speech give you the right to verbally attack groups or nations? In Germany, the neo-nazis routinely use the Internet to plan their attacks and to share propaganda. In the US, the various militias have a presence on the Internet. As people, we may cluck our tongues about the psychological balance of some of our fellow citizens. As teachers, we have to worry about children downloading the ravings of some backwoods commissar and taking the tracts home. The stuff is out there and we certainly don't want it coming into our classrooms.

Responses

We have a responsibility as caretakers to shelter our students from the evils of the world. We may not be able to filter out every evil in their lives, but from eight to three thirty we have to make every effort to separate children from the nastier influences out there. What can we do?

One response by districts is to create an Acceptable Use Policy and make sure it is distributed to students. One of the more complete policies is that of the Greenfield Central School in Indiana. Here are portions of their policy.

Board Policy on Internet Use

Application for Account and Terms and Conditions for Internet Use

Please read the following carefully before signing the attached contract.

Internet access is now available to students and teachers in Greenfield-Central Community School Corporation. We are very pleased to bring this access to Greenfield-Central and believe the Internet offers vast, diverse, and unique resources to both students and teachers. Our goal in providing this service to teachers and students is to promote educational excellence in the Greenfield-Central Schools by facilitating resource sharing, innovation, and communication.

With access to computers and people all over the world also comes the availability of material that may not be considered to be of educational value in the context of the school setting. Greenfield-Central has taken available precautions, which are limited, to restrict access to controversial materials. Greenfield-Central High School will be using Cyberpatrol, a software program, to restrict access to some locations. Other schools in the Greenfield-Central School system will rely on teacher supervision to control access (since at this time they will have no more than one connection available at any one time) . However, on a global network it is impossible to control all materials and an industrious user may discover controversial information.

These guidelines are provided here so that you are aware of the responsibilities you are about to acquire. In general this requires efficient, ethical and legal utilization of the network resources. If a Greenfield-Central user violates any of these provisions, his or her account with CougarNet will be terminated and future access may be denied, and disciplinary action will result.

CougarNet--Terms and Conditions

1) Acceptable Use--The purpose of the Internet is to support research and education in and among academic institutions in the U.S. by providing access to unique resources and the opportunity for collaborative work. The use of your account must be in support of education and research and consistent with the educational objectives of the Greenfield-Central Community School Corporation. Use of other organization's networks or computing resources must comply with the rules appropriate for that network. Transmission of any material in violation of any U.S. or state regulation is prohibited. This includes, but is not limited to: copyrighted material, threatening material, or obscene or sexually explicit material.

2) Privileges--The use of CougarNet is a privilege, not a right, and inappropriate use will result in a cancellation of those privileges. (Each student who receives an account will be part of a discussion with a Greenfield-Central faculty member pertaining to the proper use of the network.) Based upon the acceptable use guidelines outlined in this document, the system administrators will deem what is inappropriate use and their decision is final. Also, the system administrators may close an account at any time as required. The administration, faculty, and staff of Greenfield-Central may request the system administrator to deny, revoke, or suspend specific user accounts.

3) Netiquette--You are expected to abide by the generally accepted rules of network etiquette. These include (but are not limited to) the following:

- Be polite. Do not write or send abusive messages to others. Use appropriate language. Do not swear, use vulgarities, or any other inappropriate language. Do not distribute pornography, obscene or sexually explicit materials.

- Do not reveal your personal address or phone number or those of other students or colleagues.

- Note that electronic mail (email) is not guaranteed to be private. People who operate the system do have access to all mail. Messages relating to or in support of illegal activities may be reported to the authorities.

- Do not use the network in such a way that you would disrupt the use of the network by other users (e.g. downloading huge files during prime time; sending mass email messages).

- All communications and information accessible via the network should be assumed to be private property.

4) Students will not respond to unsolicited on-line contact

5) Security--Security on any computer system is a high priority, especially when the system involves many users. If you feel you can identify a security problem on CougarNet or on any Internet access, you must notify a system administrator or e-mail (postmaster@gcsc.k12.in.us). Do not demonstrate the problem to other users. Do not use another individual's account. Do not give your password to any other individual. Attempts to log in to the system as any other user will result in cancellation of user privileges. Attempts to login to CougarNet as a system administrator will result in cancellation of user privileges. Any user identified as a security risk or having a history of problems with other computer systems may be denied access to CougarNet.

6) Vandalism--Vandalism will result in cancellation of privileges. Vandalism is defined as any malicious attempt to harm or destroy data of another user, CougarNet, or any of the above listed agencies or other networks that are connected to CSN, or the NSFNet Internet backbone. This includes, but is not limited to, the uploading or creation of computer viruses.

7) It is possible for students to purchase goods and services via the Internet, and that these purchases could potentially result in unwanted financial obligations. This activity will be prohibited on access through the Greenfield-Central Schools CougarNet.

8) Students will not be allowed to subscribe to listservs or news groups unless specific permission is provided by the parent/guardian in writing and the teacher.

9) Updating Your User Information--CougarNet may occasionally require new registration and account information from you to continue the service.

You must notify CougarNet of any changes in your account information (address, etc.). Currently, there are no user fees for this service.

10) Exception of Terms and Conditions--All terms and conditions as stated in this document are applicable to the Greenfield-Central Community School Corporation. These terms and conditions reflect the entire agreement of the parties and supersede all prior oral or written agreements and understandings of the parties. These terms and conditions shall be governed and interpreted in accordance with the laws of the State of Indiana, United States of America.

11) The school corporation will not be held liable for:

- Information stored on school corporation diskettes, hard drives, or servers

- Information retrieved through the school corporation computers, networks, or on-line resources

- Personal property used to access school corporation computers, networks, or on-line resources

- Unauthorized financial obligations resulting from use of school corporation resources and accounts to access the Internet.

Any Greenfield-Central Community School Corporation student or employee may apply for an Internet account. To do so you must complete the attached contract and application. Students should return the contract to the person from whom they received the contract.

Students and their parents are required to sign the contract above before they are given an Internet account. The contract is long, but it is complete. It explains everything that is permissible and everything that is not, and makes it clear that the district takes these matters seriously.

In classrooms that have just a single line to the Internet, supervision can be somewhat simpler. Teachers make clear what can be done and what shouldn't be done, and then visually supervise the screen of the one computer that can reach the outside world. But, of course, the minute you move to a network this method of supervision is no longer possible.

Ultimately, we face the problem that the Internet gives students freedoms that they may not be ready for, and exposes them to a world that isn't as we would like it. Making very clear statements about acceptable use of this resource, and enforcing those statements, may be the only way to overcome the problematic side of the Internet.

PROJECT SUGGESTIONS

🖱 Ask others for a copy of their district's telecommunications plan. Compare two or three plans. What are the strengths and weaknesses of each? If you were going to develop a plan for your district, what parts would you keep? What process would you use?

🖱 Show the Greenfield Central Acceptable Use Policy to other teachers who have used the Internet. Are all problem areas covered in the policy, or are there other issues not resolved? Show the policy to administrators in your district. Does it seem to cover all the legal areas they fear? Find other policies on the Web. Jan Wee's page has a number of them. Her URL is:

http://www.state.wi.us/agencies/dpi/www/jans_bkm.html

Write a policy of your own that would meet the needs of your district.

🖱 Can you turn the problems of the Net into a teaching opportunity? How would you bring these issues to a class of high school students? What would you say? What materials would you share? How would you place issues of harassment and ethnic hatred in a context? Could you bring in other teachers to help? What would a unit plan for this look like?

🖳 DISCUSSION QUESTIONS

1. Even the best committee can somehow get off track. What committees have worked best in your experience? Which have had trouble? Are there some characteristics that seem to separate the successful ones from the failures?

2. What wiring efforts are underway in your district? What problems have you encountered? What model (LAN or WAN) are you using?

3. What costs are you experiencing for telecommunications? How much is going for support and training?

4. Identify a strategy that seems to be working for your school or district. How are you building interest from parents and the community in telecommunications?

5. Have you had a case where a student downloaded pornographic material? What did you do? Is this an issue parents are concerned about? What are they saying?

6. What kind of language are you finding students using on the Net? Are there specific times or events that seem to encourage them to go over the edge? What did you do about it?

7. Have you seen hate literature on the Net? Do you know of students who are going to those Net sites?

8. Does your district have an acceptable use policy? If so, how does it compare to the one of Greenfield Central? Who created your policy? Who is responsible for disciplining students who are caught violating the policy?

RECOMMENDED READING

Rothstein, R. and McKnight, L. Architecture and Costs of Connecting Schools to the NII. *THE Journal,* October 1995, 23:91-96.

The complete acceptable use policy of the Greenfield Central Schools is on the World Wide Web at URL: http://gcsc.k12.in.us/AUP/AUP.html

Chapter 13
International Perspectives:
Who's On-line, Who's Not

 **OVERVIEW**

One of the best aspects of the Internet is that it can connect us to people and places all over the world. We want our students to talk directly to their peers in China, Russia, Africa. Can they? The world has a very unequal distribution of phones and computers. By following phone lines, we should be able to see where our students can travel digitally, and where they can't.

CONNECTIVITY STATISTICS

What's lovely about the Internet is to be able to click on a World Wide Web button and be in France, looking through the Louvre. Click on another button, and you are touring the White House. Click on a third and you are in England. This is pretty heady stuff. One minute I am in Wisconsin, the next I am anywhere in the world. Suddenly geography stops having any meaning. Now

I can be a digital presence anywhere in the world just by using my magic computer.

Or can I? Those of you in rural Wisconsin already know something about technical barriers. It all looks easy on TV, but when you try to hook up your classroom, suddenly you realize not every place is equipped. Well, what's it like in the rest of the world? Who is hooked up, and who isn't?

Let's look at that issue, not just because it is a good lesson in modern economics, but because it also has a very immediate connection to my classroom. Schools that aren't wired are schools my students can't talk to. The Internet Society tries to maintain information about who's on the Net and who's not. To illustrate the connectivity of various countries around the world, they regularly update a world map showing which countries have access to the Net (Figure 13-1).

The map shows that most of the world has Internet access, but there are many countries, especially in Africa, where access is more limited. I spent the 1993-94 school year teaching at the University of Namibia in South Western Africa, so I know something about access limitations. In fact, my experience tells me that things are actually much worse than they appear on the map.

One of the problems with the map is the fact that if Internet access is available at any one place in a country, the entire nation is color coded to show Internet access. In the case of Namibia, we could get Internet access to one part of the national university. That was it. But the entire country is shaded. It appears it is now possible to get a line to the Internet anywhere. There are a number of reasons why this isn't true. Let's start with telephone access.

TELEPHONE AVAILABILITY

A quick way to see how much electronic access is possible to any country is to look at the number of phone lines they have. Here are the numbers for a few countries around the world. The wide differences between countries hints at some of the problems we face in trying to link our classrooms to others around the world.

Internet Society Connectivity Map--1995

http://info.isoc.org:80/images/mapv14.gif

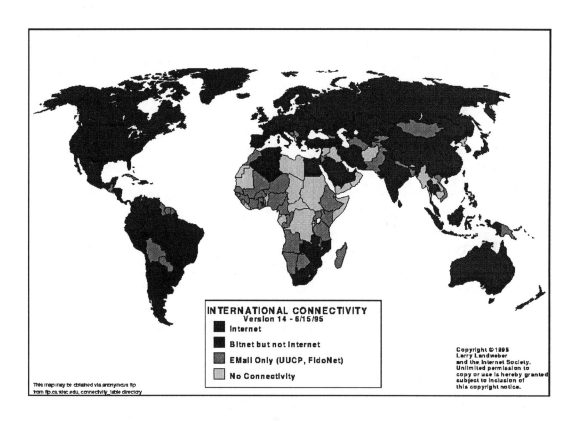

Figure 13-1

Country	Lines /100 Population
United States	51
Sweden	68
Switzerland	58
Canada	57
Denmark	57
Finland	53

The following countries have less than 1 line per 100 population:

China	India
Kenya	Nicaragua
Pakistan	Philippines
Sri Lanka	Zimbabwe

The differences are overwhelming and underline an important point--most of the world has no access to phones. If they don't have phones, how are we going to link our computers to theirs?

Why are there so few phones in the developing world? One of the principal factors is cost. Because much of the developing world is rural, its phones are state-owned, and its technology is old, the average phone user there pays far higher phone charges than we are used to. All these charges are evident in the cost of using electronic mail. Here is a comparison between the US and Zambia:

Internet Costs

United States	about $2 per hour
Zambia	$100 connect fee
	$40 monthly fee
	$10 traffic fee

Relative Income	US is 100 times Zambia
Relative Cost	Zambia pays 1000 to 3000 times US costs

This huge disparity in costs means that there are insurmountable barriers in getting Internet connections to more than a fraction of the people in the developing world. They simply have to pay too much.

CONSEQUENCES FOR
INTERNATIONAL COMMUNICATION

So what does this mean to me when I try to link my class in Wisconsin to the classroom of someone in the developing world? There are at least four consequences:

1. Few connections in developing world
2. Few connections outside of urban elite
3. Connection quality limits use of graphics
4. Computer quality can interrupt communications

First, it will be harder for me to find such connections. There aren't as many African or Chinese classes on line as there are American classes on line. As much as I may want to make contact with them, there may not be enough people at the other end of the line to make that possible.

If I do make the connection, I should know I will seldom be connecting with the average child in that country. Phone connections are concentrated in the major cities and are available to those schools with the resources to fund them. In short, if I make a link at all, it will likely be to the urban rich. The chance that I could link a rural school in Wisconsin with a rural school in Zimbabwe is virtually nil. It would be an exciting communication if I could achieve it, but I would have to overcome a long list of problems.

If I do make a connection, it will be for text only. I can do email. Text is not very demanding. Even if the people at the other end have slow modems, we should be able to get messages to them. But graphics are out of the question. Scanning the photos of my students and sending them through just requires too much telecommunications capacity. Any connections we make will be at the lowest possible denominator.

We should also expect breakdowns and silences. Getting a message there and back will take time to begin with. But computer resources are also more vulnerable to breakdown. There is no Radio Shack on the corner, nor is there Fed Ex to bring in new parts. Meanwhile, they fight heat, humidity, and power spikes. Keeping their machines up and running is a constant demand for patience and resourcefulness. You and I shouldn't be too annoyed if they don't seem to get back to us as quickly as we would like.

REASONS TO MAKE THE EFFORT

Given these problems, it would be tempting to say, well, let's just talk to Europeans and leave the developing world alone. That would be easy, but painful to the developing world. They need and want connections to the rest of us. They understand the consequences for those who are left out of the information age. The point is summed up nicely by Mathiea Ekra, Minister of State, the Ivory Coast:

> *Those who have recently achieved their independence must take care this time not to miss the last train of the twentieth century.*

Information is the last train of the twentieth century. If you feel left out living in a small town in Wisconsin, imagine how people feel living in a small town in the Kalahari. They want this link, and will put in far more work than you have to in order to make the link happen.

BUIDLING QUALITY INTO GLOBAL COMMUNICATION

How do we ensure that we get the most out of these links? Let's look at common information exchanges and the kinds of problems that can exist. I will use much of my own experience as an example, since I linked my students at the University of Namibia to my former students at the University of Wisconsin-Stevens Point, and did just about everything wrong. Here's what I did--don't do these!

Delays

First, it seems like everything takes too long. Messages may travel at thousands of miles per second, but then they have to wait in a router or in a network server. The system we used in Africa was called "store and forward," meaning the messages sat for 12 hours until we dialed up and downloaded them. This saved us the cost of a leased line, but, of course, meant that messages arrived more than 12 hours after they were sent. We also used a different academic calendar in Africa. There are different holidays, different seasons, a different school year.

The result was impatience on both ends. Add to that students who don't check their email every day, and you've got breaks in communication. I should have coordinated the sending and receiving of messages (and supervised that students actually did both) far more actively than I did. We also needed to warn students that answers would take days, not hours.

Ignorance

The first question most of my students in America sent my students in Africa was, "Where is Namibia?" It would appear none of the university students in America could locate a library or a map. Besides demonstrating for the nth time that Americans live on the world's biggest island, that question and the others that followed just wasted time. Such questions also wasted money. The University in Namibia had to pay for every second of time it was connected to the phones. Downloading nonsense from America was not a good use of their limited resources. All it would have taken was some initial classroom instruction in geography, history, and weather, and much of the first three rounds of email messages could have been eliminated.

Insensitivity

Some of the questions from America weren't just dumb, they were rude. I walked into the computer lab at the University of Namibia one day to find four of my students obviously upset about a message they had just received. The author had asked, "Are there schools in Africa?" The fact that he was sending a message to a university in Africa might have given him some clue, but he missed it. This and similar messages gave the Namibian students the impression that Americans have no respect for them at all. One asked me, "Do they think we live in trees?"

This problem might have been eliminated if the American students had made some effort to study southern Africa, if the teachers on the American end of the line had screened messages before they went out, or if the American students had asked themselves, "How would I feel if someone asked *me* this question?" A bit of role playing might have helped.

Triviality

We assume that connecting students ten thousand miles from each other will automatically lead to intercultural insight. It seems a reasonable assumption, but it is wrong. What do students say to total strangers on the other side of the globe? Not very much. This is totally new to everyone involved, and so too often results in little content and little insight. Unless shaped and developed, many of the email conversations you witness resemble the conversations we have with total strangers--mumbled platitudes about the weather.

CONNECTING THROUGH PROJECTS

How can we avoid these pitfalls and make the intercultural connection worth the huge efforts required by teachers and students at the other end? Successful projects seem to involve collegiality and common efforts. One of the most successful conversations involved two nursing students. They were both interested in AIDS prevention and shared a common professional background. Within two messages they were treating each other like colleagues, were respectful, and were both benefiting from information channels that were otherwise closed to them.

Discussion of technology also seemed to work. Students can quickly find common ground in technology that is available worldwide, and problems that occur worldwide. They can share technical expertise and appreciate each other's skills.

An area that is more problematic is ecology. Students have an interest here, but tend to demonize those with other views. American students may be shocked that there are people who find killing baby seals perfectly acceptable, and believe culling elephant herds is a sensible action. Seven hundred thousand people went into the Wisconsin woods last fall trying to kill a deer, but those same people might feel differently about different people killing different animals. We adults differ widely on when, if, or how, it is appropriate to kill animals. It may be asking too much for children to discuss this topic without getting hurt feelings.

CONNECTING POINTS

Making connections to developing nations may be difficult, but it is important both to our students and to theirs. Here are several Web sites that can give you information about schools on the Web:

Intercultural E-Mail Classroom Connections
http://www.stolaf.edu/network.iecc

Electronic Schoolbook (for South Africa)
http://www.icon.co.za/~matthew/schoolza.html

Western Cape School Network (South Africa)
http://www.wcape.school.za

Eastern Cape School Network (South Africa)
http://www.ecape.school.za

Web66 International Schools Registry
http://web66.coled.umn.edu

DISCUSSION QUESTIONS

1. Have you made an Internet connection to a developing nation? How did you make that connection? Have you run into any technical hurdles?

2. How do you prepare students before they contact people in another country? What would you want them to know?

3. Do you screen messages before students email them? How do you ensure quality and sensitivity?

4. What kinds of projects that your students can share equally with the students of another country would you recommend?

5. How can you hold down the costs that schools in developing nations have to pay for email?

RECOMMENDED READING

Wresch, W. (1996). *Disconnected: Haves and Have Nots in the Information Age.* New Brunswick, NJ: Rutgers University Press.

Chapter 14

Hardware: Modems, Phone Lines, and Access Points

💻 OVERVIEW

How does a message actually get from my computer to the Internet and back? What process is used? What equipment is needed? What options do I have for getting my class hooked up? Teachers may not need to be experts in digital communication, but they need some background in how the process actually works in order to know what equipment they need.

MODEMS

The principal requirement of telecommunications is that your computer somehow be linked up to a phone line. That connection is generally made by a modem--a "modulator/demodulator." What does a modulator/demodulator do? It takes the information coming out of your computer and "modulates" it. This is to say it overlays the computer signal on the phone signal. In the process it deals with such problems as analog phone lines, error codes, and transfer speeds. What does *that* mean? It has to change the signal coming out of the computer so it matches the signal used by phone lines, add error checks to determine whether the signal is arriving at the other end correctly, and send out the signal at a speed that is different from the speed of the computer. This is actually a lot of work, but it is done by boxes that usually cost under two hundred dollars.

What kinds of modems are there? There are two choices you get to make. Do you want an internal or external modem? What speed do you want it to go?

Internal Versus External Modems

Most home computers are being sold with internal modems. This means the circuitry that does the translation of the signal is all put on a printed circuit board in one of the expansion slots of the computer. The board is about three inches by four inches and is often very cheap. The only part of it that you will see is the place at the back of the computer where you can plug in a phone line.

An external modem is usually a small case about one inch high, four inches wide and six inches deep. It has one wire that goes into the computer and a place for the phone line to go. It also has a series of lights on the front. It usually costs about fifty dollars more than the internal modem.

Which would you want? There are two issues at work. One is visibility. Since an internal modem is locked away inside the computer we can't see it work. Why would we want to? Because if a connection breaks down, you will want to know where the break occurred. If you have an external modem, you can look at the lights on the front and at least see that the equipment on your end is still working. This may sound like a small thing, but it takes only one frustrating afternoon trying to make a difficult connection and you will be glad to pay the extra money for a modem you can actually see work.

The second issue is portability. At school there may be more than one computer you would like to connect to the Internet. The principal may have one machine that she hooks to the net, and the librarian may have another machine that she wants to wheel into the principal's office to connect. If you have an internal modem in one computer, it will only work in that computer (unless you are prepared to pull the computer apart to get it out). An external modem can stay right where it is. You unplug it from one computer and plug it into another, and you have your connection.

Speeds

The current standard for modems is 14,400 bits per second. Since it takes ten bits to encode a letter of the alphabet, such a modem is sending 1,440 characters per second. That is roughly one page of text per second--not bad. Where troubles arise is with graphic images. Pictures that take a million bytes would need 694 seconds to transfer (ten million bits divided by 14,400 bits). 694 seconds is more than ten minutes. That's not acceptable.

What can I do? I can go with a faster modem. An increasing number of 28,800 bps modems are available. They go twice as fast; I wait half as long. The only catch may be the local phone lines. The faster I go, the more chance that a "noisy" local line will introduce an error. In rural areas, lines were installed to let people talk to people, not to funnel megabits of data. The upgrading of rural lines is going to take years.

What can you do about the speed problem? One is to avoid graphics. There is a huge amount of information out there in text form. Just keeping up with that information will keep most of us busy. What else? You can buy a direct link between your school and an Internet provider. Now you can get speeds from 56,000 bits per second to 1.5 million bps. But, before we talk about those wires, let's talk about the local wires in your school building.

PREMISES WIRING

A large number of districts are in the process of rewiting their buildings. Some are putting phone lines in all the classrooms, some are putting in network connections, a few are doing both. There are professional consultants that examine buildings for optimum wiring configurations, so we don't need to worry about the details of all this. But there are two technical aspects of this wiring that teachers may need to understand.

One is "attenuation." Signals weaken over distance. The wiring puts up some resistance and gradually wears the signal down. For computers linked to a local area network, the rough limit is 600 feet before some kind of signal booster is necessary. The result is that if you are at the end of a long hallway, you may face some extra hurdles in getting your classroom connected.

The second problem is "noise." While we usually think of classroom noise as what students do at the end of the hour, this kind of "noise" is what machines do to electrical circuits around them. When a motor comes on it can send out an electromagnetic spike that overwhelms the information coming down a phone line. If you and I were talking, we might just hear a little static. But a computer signal might have its contents changed or obliterated. Again, the problem isn't common, but if you happen to be in the Tech Ed wing of the building, or run a line next to the air conditioner, you may have problems.

PHONE LINES

You have several options on how you connect to the Internet. As you might expect, each approach involves trade-offs between cost and convenience.

Direct Connections

This approach is the top of the line. It gives you a dedicated line between your school and some internet provider. What's more, this line is usually fast-- 56,000 bps to 1.5 million bps (T-1), so graphics come flying. Rather than paying for each call, you pay a flat fee each month (but this can be hundreds of dollars). On your end, you install an Internet router. This is a computer dedicated to sending messages back and forth on the Internet. This is the computer where you would install your own World Wide Web pages. It is also the computer that would distribute messages to other machines in your building or across your district. Since you now have your own router on the Internet, you now also have your own address (www.myschool.edu).

How much is this going to cost you? Robert Blocher of Wisconsin's Department of Public Instruction estimates the initial cost for the line and computer will be $4,000 to $7,000. But you also need to make ongoing payments to the phone company and your Internet provider, so figure another $3,000 annually. This is probably more than your PTO can cover with cookie sales, but it is amazing how many Wisconsin schools are finding the money somewhere.

Dial-up SLIP/PPP

Now we are back to making individual phone calls to connect to the Internet, but at least we are accessing the Internet directly. SLIP stands for Serial Line Internet Protocol, and PPP means Point-to-Point Protocol. We could probably now go on a digression about what "protocol" means, but in essence it is just a term for a technical agreement that everyone will send information in the same order and in the same form. It is like our general agreement to address letters with the person's name first, and state and zip code last.

The important part of SLIP and PPP is that the protocol we are using is the Internet protocol. Our computer has to be running software that knows how to put messages in the Internet format. If we have that software (usually less than $50), our machine can send out and receive information like any other station on the Internet. We can get all the information that we would via a direct link, but we get it more slowly.

Dial-up SLIP is not a bad initial option for schools. You only pay for the time you are connected to the phone lines, so you can put some limits on your expenses, and while you do not get blazing speed, you at least get enough service to get some of the flavor of the Internet.

Dial-up Commercial

A third option is to dial up a national email service like America Online or CompuServe, and let them serve as a gateway to the Internet. They each provide their own resources (America Online has extensive discussion lists of its own for teachers and students), but they understand that the market is demanding Internet access, so they will provide that as well.

This leads us to the next link in the chain--the Internet Service Provider (ISP).

ACCESS POINTS: THE ISP

It seems logical that there be someone at the other end of the phone line. These are the Internet Service Providers who will connect you to the Net. This is a rapidly growing cottage industry. Nearly every small town has some entrepreneur who has leased a high speed phone line, bought a modem pool, and can now link people to the Net.

Two or three years ago, before the emergence of this industry, schools connected to the Internet by calling their local university. This is becoming less common as more alternatives become available and as universities become wary of competing with private enterprise (which is illegal in Wisconsin).

How do you find out about service providers in your area? These days most are in the yellow pages. The harder problem is selecting which ISP to use. Bob Bocher of Wisconsin's DPI makes these recommendations for questions you might ask:

- *What is the installation fee?*
- *What are the monthly charges?*
- *What are the hourly charges?*
- *Do they have a help desk?*
- *What hours is help available?*
- *What training is included in their fees?*
- *Can they give you the names of others who use them?*

PROJECT SUGGESTIONS

🖰 If you were going to teach telecommunications processes to students, what materials would you use? What topics would you include? How would you illustrate the processes?

🖰 Create a plan to put your school directly on the Internet. Work out a budget for both initial and ongoing expenses. Make a recommendation for both the hardware and software for your local router. How would you link the router to other machines in your building? How would you put Web pages on the router? What kind of ongoing personnel needs would you have? What kind of staff training would you do?

Discussion Questions

1. What kind of modems do you have in your school? Why did you choose those?

2. What policy does your school have about classroom phone lines? When is the last time that policy was reviewed?

3. How much would it cost for your school to have a direct connection to the Internet? Be sure to include both initial and monthly charges.

4. What ISPs are available locally? What range of services do they provide? Contact each for rate sheets.

RECOMMENDED READING

Bocher, R. Accessing the Internet: Options and Issues. Wisconsin Department of Public Instruction. Call (608) 266-2127 for a copy. Bocher also has a number of other publications on Internet providers.

Chapter 15
Access: Getting to the Net

 OVERVIEW

One of the biggest problems of the Internet is just getting to it. How can teachers arrange for the phone lines and access charges that are required? Fortunately, there are numerous simultaneous efforts underway to make Internet more accessible.

THE PROBLEM

A recent front page photo in the *Chronicle of Higher Education* showed a long line of students at the University of Texas waiting to get access to a computer. During the course of interviews students explained how important it was for them to get to a computer to write their research papers at the end of the semester, and how angry they were that the lines were so long. The lines weren't long two years ago. It has been ten years since universities have experienced this kind of problem. Then, in the initial crunch of computer use in the early 1980s, the problem was also bad. Some universities threw up their hands and decided students should buy their own computers when they came to campus. Most universities muddled along and gradually built up fairly large computer labs that seemed to handle most student demand.

Then came Internet. Now a new surge of students hit the labs, wanting both word processors to write papers and access to the World Wide Web to do their research. Then there were students who just wanted to send email to everyone in the world, and others who just wanted to surf. Add it all up, and there are too many students spending too many hours on limited numbers of machines. So colleges are buried again. Nobody is happy, everybody thinks somebody ought to do something.

We also have exactly the same process hitting America's high schools. We had just about worked out a large enough set of computer labs so English had theirs and Math had theirs and not too many toes were stepped on, and now everyone is trying to get to the one lab that has limited access to the Net. It looks like 1985 all over again. Here are some recent Internet access figures (Bocher, 1995):

Internet Access
- US colleges and universities: 90%
- US public libraries: 20.9%
- US K-12 public schools: 35%

Unfortunately, access is really worse than these numbers indicate. They show a school as having access if one line is present in the building. We all know how little help we get from just one line. Full integration of the Internet will come only when we have access in every classroom, and only a tiny portion of schools have that. What can we do about this situation? There are several solutions in the works.

AVENUES OF ACCESS

How do we get our schools hooked to the Net? Besides the efforts of local schools, there are several larger efforts underway that we should know about and encourage.

National Initiatives

There is clearly an explosion of activity at the national level. The government is at work on a variety of fronts, but so is the private sector. Let's look at how their actions may improve Internet access in our classrooms, starting with the government.

Vice President Al Gore is usually given the credit for coining the term "Information Superhighway," and pushing for both a National Information Infrastructure (NII) and a Global Information Infrastructure (GII). Gore's initiatives also include five principles:

- Encouraging investment in the NII
- Promoting and protecting competition
- Providing open access to the NII by consumers and service providers
- Preserving and advancing universal service to avoid information "haves" and "have nots"
- Ensuring flexibility so the NII can keep change with technological and market changes (Bocher).

Work on the NII is being pursued by the Information Infrastructure Task Force in conjunction with the Commerce Department's National Telecommunications and Information Administration.

Concurrent with this NII activity is legislative action on telecommunications reform. There is considerable disagreement over how much federal oversight should exist in the telecommunications industry. Should the market be given free reign? This might encourage competition, but what if one or two major players win control and then set prices commensurate with a monopoly position? What about protections for the poor and elderly? Under tenets of universal access, basic phone service was provided at less than true costs to the user, while larger companies paid more than their true costs to balance the situation. In effect, the rich underwrote phone service to the poor. If we are going to end that subsidy for the poor, what will we do about the elderly who might need a phone line to call an ambulance? Will there also be no subsidy for schools and libraries?

The Telecommunications Deregulation Act is a major piece of legislation that emphasizes competing interests and competing philosophies about government's proper role in the marketplace. It will have a significant impact on the telecommunications environment we work in. Combine that legislation with NII efforts, and you get more activity out of Washington than has occurred in this area in decades.

All of the government activity is complicated by a totally new level of commercial activity. This activity centers around the phrase "emerging and converging." You will hear the phrase many times when people discuss technological and business developments in this field. What is emerging? New ways of moving information. What is converging? Businesses and technologies that used to be distinct. Take your local cable TV company. That wire coming into your house brings TV shows. But there is room on it (bandwidth) to bring in phone calls also. But two can play that game. Once your phone line is optical fiber there is plenty of bandwidth for phone conversations, stock market reports, and first run movies to come down the wire. Cable companies and phone companies are converging.

Who else is converging at that phone box coming into your home or your classroom?

1. *Computer hardware/ software companies:* Why shouldn't Microsoft handle home banking software as well as other software?
2. *TV studios:* Is there a good reason why Disney shouldn't ship products directly down your phone line?
3. *Cable TV:* Why not call grandma on the cable?
4. *Phone companies:* Voice traffic uses so little capacity on the line. Add Internet, add MGM movies?
5. *Consumer electronics firms:* Is Game Boy the ATM of the future?
6. *Publishing companies:* Books are on-line, multimedia products are coming: Can we take courses at Prentice-Hall University?
7. *Broadcast networks:* Turner Network classic movies over the Internet?

Meanwhile AT&T is requesting the right to go back into the local phone business, competing with the former baby bells--Ameritech, Bell Atlantic, etc. To make their presence felt in schools, AT&T announced November 1, 1995 that they would give every school in the country 100 hours of free Internet connect time. Not a bad way to announce "We're back."

What an interesting time! You can't tell the players without a score card. All we know for sure is that there are far more players than we are used to thinking about, all of them competing for our business under rules that are changing every day. Pass the Maalox. We do have educational leaders trying to watch all this action and give us a half-time score, but we have to give all the experts a break on this one. The situation is changing too fast for anyone to be certain where things are headed. All we can do is try our best to keep up. Fortunately, things are a little more stable at the state level.

State Initiatives

In July 1994 the Wisconsin Legislature passed Wisconsin Act 496 calling for the creation of an *Advanced Telecommunications Foundation*. This is a significant act that will make large sums of money available for Internet access. The Foundation has two funds, an endowment fund of 40.5 million dollars, and a fast start fund of 10 million dollars. These are both brand new funds and are just establishing how this money will be disbursed, but they have already created five basic directions for where the money can be used:

1. Establishing a clearinghouse of potential projects
2. Cooperative projects between telecommunication users and providers
3. Projects that promote effective use of the telecommunications infrastructure
4. Projects that assist individuals in applying information
5. Projects or programs that educate consumers (Bocher)

Also, as part of this activity, Ameritech will invest $700 million over the next five years to bring optical fiber to every high school, middle school, and public library in its service area.

There is nothing special about Wisconsin. Every state has some venture among developed between telephone companies, the state government, and public schools. Some are more formal thanthe effort in Wisconsin, some are less. In every case the effort is the same--to get Internet capacity into the schools and into rural corners of the state.

Netday

An interesting mix of state and national efforts is NetDay. Begun in California, NetDay is now appearing in state after state. What is Netday? Here are a few press descriptions:

Yes, NetDay is actually here.

Thousands of volunteers are climbing out of cyberspace and onto real school campuses from one end of the state to the other. Parents, teachers, local businesspeople, technicians, and even the President of the United States are meeting each other for the first time pulling cable.

"In Oakland, we are just smiling, smiling, smiling!" said Libby Schaaf, who has been coordinating volunteers through the Marcus A. Foster Educational Institute. "The community response to this event is unbelievable! We've had so many volunteers, we've had to turn people away. And it's not like the volunteers are from one big company. This is people coming out one by one, each hearing about NetDay in a different way."

Fifty schools in Oakland alone are being wired as this dispatch is being sent out. At one school, the Visual and Performing Arts Academy, volunteers showed up to find every bulletin plastered with welcome messages made by students. The patience award goes to volunteers at Hillcrest Elementary School, where the person who was supposed to open up the school was sent into last-minute strike negotiations. Volunteers had to wait for two hours until someone showed up. At last report, however, humor was still high.

And, speaking of strike negotiations, NetDay is making unprecedented history in the labor movement as both sides in the bitter Oakland teachers' strike called off their labor dispute so NetDay could go on. At most schools, striking and non-striking teachers are working alongside principals and volunteers.

Not to mention Bill Clinton, the President of the United States, and VP Al Gore, who were pulling cable at San Ygnacio Valley High School in Concord this morning. Says John Gage, NetDay organizer, who was on hand for the event: "President Clinton is now a Category 5 installer." John, who is Sun Microsystems' top scientist in real life, handed Clinton three spools of red, white and blue cable on a mop handle he brought from home.

Clinton and Gore pulled wire down from the conduit, Clinton punched down the cable into the Cat-5 jack, and then both of them signed the jack in the school's computer lab. The first-ever Clinton/Gore information port.

Then, there was the four-way teleconference featuring top administration officials: Clinton/Gore in Concord, Commerce Secy Ron Brown in Sacramento, FCC chair Reed Hunt in Los Angeles, and Education Secy Richard Riley in San Diego.

But, as we all know, not everything goes right the first time. Well, at least Ron Brown and Clinton could chat in cyberspace. Clinton, who wore khakis and workshoes for the event, took time out to tease Brown for showing up to wire a school in a suit. "Nobody ever told me there was a dress code," Brown jibed back.

Netday's not all work. Tonight, a massive party is being held at Kaiser Arena in Oakland (capacity 7,900). Free beer (Yes, you heard it right.) And lots of free food. Kids have cooked up 1,000 cupcakes and arranged them in the shape of the NetDay logo. The party is being arranged on last-minute notice by Kiwanian Linda Kiehle. Come watch the events on giant screens. Bring a pot luck dish if you're nearby. Don't even think of ordering pizza delivered tonight; seems most of the pizza parlors all over the Bay Area are sending their own NetDay specials to the arena.

Yes, even the President and Vice President went to California to pull cable (at least briefly). Al Gore summed up the effort this way: "The new challenge for America is this: As we enter the 21st century, every young person should enter the workforce technologically literate. Last September, President Clinton and I announced NetDay 96, a volunteer effort to connect California's schools to the network. The long-term goal is to provide worldwide Internet access to every California student and teacher. On NetDay 96, the immediate goal is to solve one part of the problem: Connect as many California schools as possible to the Information Superhighway"

NetDay is, of course, part photo-op for local politicians, but it does help build support for internetworking activities and does also connect some classrooms. Is there a down side to this free labor and public support? Yes. Some union locals have been nervous about amateurs pulling wire around school buildings and at least one electrician's local has made its opposition public. So you may want to check with everyone in your school before you add your support to what is a growing national effort.

Local Initiatives

We can pick up our daily paper and see that a great deal is happening nationally and internationally in the telecommunications field. But all of this can be remote for the science teacher who wants to connect to NASA today. It is nice that Washington is talking about the issue--it would be nicer if there were an Internet connection in the back of the classroom already. What can individual teachers do while the high fliers of commerce and government sort all this out?

First, of course, you need to be sure someone in your district is watching for state moneys and connecting with telephone company initiatives. There *is* money in the state for Internet initiatives. But people with money rarely walk through your door and hand it to you. Someone in your district will have to watch for the calls for proposals, fill in the grant applications, and establish a contact person at the local telephone company. Have you determined who that person will be?

A second effort that districts need to make is to find friends in the community who also need Internet services. One of the problems for rural schools is that the local phone lines and switching technology may be out of date for handling digital communications. The community may also be some distance from the closest Internet POP (Point of Presence). That means you need to cover long distance charges to that POP. The consequence is that remote schools often face higher charges for worse service than their urban peers. But every business in your community faces exactly the same problem. They also are paying higher fees for poorer service. You have an ally.

You may have many allies. Your public library wants Internet access, as does the local hospital. Businesses of any size are currently putting much of their billing on networks and handling more and more paperwork electronically through electronic data interchange (EDI) systems. The Internet is not a direct player in EDI, but a network is a network and anything that gets optical fiber to your door is a help.

Small businesses may have far more presence on the Net than you may suppose. Century 21 now shows houses on its World Wide Web sites. Retailers on Main Street can buy a "turn-key" Web computer that gives them all the hardware and software they need to get onto the Web. Others are renting space on machines being provided by the equivalent of Internet advertising agencies. Have a group of high school students do a research project on the Web and local business. In one week they could do a survey that would tell you who is now on, and who is getting on. I guarantee the number is larger than you think.

Provide a service to your new friends. Web pages are written in a "language" called Hypertext Markup Language (HTML). Any kid who can program in BASIC can create a Web page. Why not create pages for area businesses? That's what John Gravelle's students do at Merrill High School. Bring in some art students to help with graphic design, and you can produce pages that look as good as anything coming from Madison Avenue (recent studies are showing that businesses are bypassing traditional advertising providers and going to the Web directly). You now have businesses in town who want your school on the Net because it is important to their own bottom line.

All of this can get a POP in your community. If you can save on long distance charges to the Internet, so can all the businesses in town, and everyone is happy. (Don't worry about the phone companies--their traffic is growing fast enough to keep them afloat). Have you solved all your problems? No, but you have taken care of an annoying piece of the puzzle.

What can you do inside your building? Begin by looking at where your phone lines are now. One grade school teacher (whom I shall not name) connected to the Net each day by having three of her students wheel a computer on a cart down to the principal's office to plug in there. After several months of this the principal decided she should have a line of her own in her room and had it installed. Not a bad strategy. Not only did she demonstrate to the principal that hooking to the Internet was something students could and would do regularly, but by depriving the principal of a phone line part of each day she gave the principal added motivation to get another line installed.

Librarians are also good resources. Many already have a phone line in their room. That's a pretty good start. They also tend to know more about on-line resources than the rest of us. Their profession deals daily with on-line card catalogs and huge databases. Furthermore, they may be looking for allies as desperately as you are. They may not have enough resources to help all the teachers and students who want to get on-line, but they can often ration out enough connectivity so that you can get started. Every teacher who logs on gives the librarian one more argument to use for another phone line, another computer, another increment in her phone budget.

The best local strategy may be to begin with the awareness that you are not alone. Find your allies; build your support base. You are not the only one in your community who needs to connect to the world.

PROJECT SUGGESTIONS

🖱 A great deal is happening at the state and national levels. Research the various telecommunications bills currently making the rounds (Remember Thomas? It is a very convenient online reference). What are their strengths and weaknesses? What do they say about education? What are the major issues that are under discussion? If you were to testify before a congressional committee on telecommunications issues, what would you say? Put together a package that would bring state teachers up to speed on this issue.

Work with one of your classes to conduct a survey of local business connectivity. What is going on in your community? What problems do they face? What role do they see for the local schools? Where do they see themselves in five years?

DISCUSSION QUESTIONS

1. What strategies did your building pioneers use to get on-line?

2. Which business in your town was the first to go on-line? What strategy did they use? What barriers did they overcome? What was their rationale for making the effort? How do they feel about it now?

3. Who has been involved in state efforts? What help is the state providing? What did you do to get involved?

Chapter 16
Future Directions:
The Next Five Years

 ## OVERVIEW

Many of the opportunities and challenges of digital information are still emerging. Decision makers need to know what is available now, but they also have to have a sense of what will be coming at them in the next few years. This chapter will look at some of the most likely developments to impact our schools.

TECHNICAL DEVELOPMENTS

John Kolman is Vice President for Advanced Products at Ameritech. His view of the future? More bandwidth. His argument goes something like this. In the past decade we have seen amazing increases in computing power. The result is grade school children often have more computing power in their bedrooms than Fortune 500 companies had in corporate headquarters twenty years ago. The technology of computing has changed in ways that are obvious to all of us.

In the meantime, we pick up the phone and call grandma in much the same way as we did half a century ago. This is odd, since in many respects the phone system is a large computer network. The machines that route calls are in fact computers. So why don't we see the kind of developments in telecommunications that we see in computers? Many factors are at work, including a huge established base of copper wire with its inherent limits, a mix of local phone companies with their own corporate inertia, and an unclear regulatory situation for the industry.

All of those problems are being resolved. Optical fiber is being laid world-wide, phone companies are responding to increased competition, and the government is giving phone companies more room to do business. The result? Bandwidth--the ability to move more information faster. It is as if the highways of America suddenly went from two lane to forty lane. There is now room for more trucks, more cars, all traveling safely at hundreds of miles an hour. When will we see this? In some respects we already are. Every time we can download an image from the Louvre, and do it in seconds, we are seeing the impact of optical fiber and digital switches.

If Kolman is right and we get the increases he is expecting, we will see not only images in seconds, but full-motion video with concert-quality sound, and it will arrive everywhere.

While general improvements in the telecommunications infrastructure will allow more information movement in general, there are two specific developments we are already seeing.

The first is a movement to multimedia--combinations of text, picture, sound, and video. Commercial Web sites like Disney are already making clips of their movies available over the Internet. The problem case is video. At thirty frames per second, movie quality images could require a transfer rate of three hundred million bits per second. By reducing image quality substantially, it is possible to get down to a million bits per second, but even that would currently require a dedicated T1 line. Both data compression strategies and bandwidth improvements are going to be required before real full-motion video becomes a reality. But the movement is in that direction, meaning that our students might not only be able to hear from arctic explorers but also be able to watch them in real-time as they race for the pole. In the meantime there are more and more video efforts underway, including video conferencing and video clips that can be transferred over time and then shown at nearly normal speed. The consequence should be ever more realism and immediacy in the information shared across the planet.

A second development is important conceptually. Sun Microsystems has developed an operating system called "Java." Java rethinks how computers on a network should interact. In the past, each computer on a network needed a complete copy of a program before it could accomplish a task. For instance, I would need a complete copy of a word processor before I could look at a word processing document you might want to send me over the Net. This is expensive for me since I have to buy the word processing program, and may be frustrating for me if I buy the program only to find out six weeks later my version is obsolete. I might be tempted to tell you to keep your word processing document to yourself.

Much the same thing is happening now with video on the Internet. Before I can view a video clip you might want to send me, I first have to buy a video viewer, but I am reluctant to do that since I know that all new technology changes quickly and the viewer I buy today may be the Beta video camera of tomorrow. Java changes the rules. It sends me the video clips and parts of the program I need to play it. Some it installs temporarily on my computer, part it runs from the sending computer. This means more information is being sent over the Net and less is sitting on my machine. As long as transfer rates are high (we are back to bandwidth here), why not use the Net and make fewer demands on my machine?

What does Java mean? If it becomes a key process in network operations, it may mean that we spend more money on faster links to the network, and less money on software loaded on our own machines. In times of highly dynamic development (like now) it could mean that we get access to cutting edge products much more quickly. We would see the latest in technology in more classrooms.

POLITICAL DEVELOPMENTS

While technological developments may give us more and faster connections, politics also has a part to play. Two recent developments, Thomas and C-SPAN, demonstrate that government can become more open. In one we get on-line access to congressional information, in the other we get live coverage of political activity. Lest we get too enthusiastic, we need to pinch ourselves and remember that the cameras are often turned in C-SPAN broadcasts so we can't see that the impassioned congressman is screeching at an empty house. And Thomas tells us nothing about what goes on behind closed doors or over drinks in Georgetown clubs.

Yet there is a general sense that the people have a right to know. And we are seeing more legislative information in places on the Web. Those wanting to explain the workings of government to children should have a growing array of artifacts they can show in class: Here is what a bill looks like--here is what your congressman said yesterday--here is the President's schedule for tomorrow.

While government becomes more transparent, the recent CompuServe pornography suit makes it clear we will have national and international action to limit what gets on the Internet. Some of the early actions seem heavy handed and could bring dangerous doses of censorship to the net. But a healthy discussion of what is acceptable in the school and in the home could take some of the more bizarre elements of the Internet out of our classrooms.

At the same time, we can expect a continuing discussion of access rights. Newt Gingrich's call for tax deductions for laptop computers is just one of the more visible moments in an ongoing debate over how we make the information highway the property of all the citizens of our nation. That debate generally centers on the cost of technology and the need to reduce the costs for those with low income. But the debate also includes discussions of training and "information literacy." The point is made that children who do not know how to drive on the information highway are disadvantaged in seeking jobs and in understanding political issues. We should expect calls from citizen groups that schools demonstrate we are making information literacy a part of the curriculum and that our graduates have proficiency in identifiable information skills.

EDUCATIONAL DEVELOPMENTS

While our schools are impacted by general changes in technology and politics, there are also specific forces that will shape the kinds of resources that are available to us on-line. Both government and business are important resources for us, but they seem to be trending in opposite directions.

Government is shrinking. One of the less positive educational developments of this trend is a reduction in resources available for education. We have levy limits in districts, major attacks on the Education Department in Washington, and pressures on state departments of education as well. Obviously all these changes affect schools in many ways. One of the ways we may not have thought about is the amount of resources available to us at the end of our phone lines. Both Wisconsin and Texas have put together a very nice Web presence. Those Web sites didn't happen by magic. Professionals had to have the time and the expertise to build them.

Because they did it, we don't have to. Need quick suggestions for what to do in social studies tomorrow? Surf the Wisconsin Department of Public Instruction Web page and you can find lots of good ideas. Can't remember what's available from NASA? Look in TENET's page. The educational leadership in Wisconsin and Texas (and every other state) is an information provider. They help make telecommunications an important educational endeavor. As they shrink, what they bring to the Net also shrinks, and so does the value of the Net.

While government fights for resources, the education industry finds its place as a resource. There is money to be made supplying schools with books, software, computers, chalk, and erasers. A growing number of companies are finding there is also money to be made supplying schools with on-line resources.

Two of the pioneers here were AT&T with its Learning Network, and

National Geographic with its Kidsnet. Both charge for their services, and both found a ready market. Now Scholastic has entered the market and more will follow. What can they sell? People and experiences. While we can get free connections to scientists at the Jet Propulsion Laboratory or NASA, would we pay so students could connect to the MVP of the Super Bowl or the CEO of Microsoft? Canada pays its Writers in Electronic Residence. Scholastic sells hours of contact with some of its authors.

And what of selling experience? Arctic Explorer was a project principally directed at crossing the North Pole. They made some contact with schools as well, but that was just one part of a larger mission. What would it take for some vendor to change priorities and go to the North Pole, not to get there, but to talk to students about getting there? In essence, we provide students with virtual electronic field trips. And we sell those trips. Pick an exotic location--the Nile, the Great Wall of China, the Amazon Rain Forest. Company X brings you daily descriptions of their travels and travails, takes your questions, and supplies you with lesson plans in a colorful ring binder.

Whether some company follows my business plan exactly or not, the general direction is clear. The quality of our interaction with the Net is based on two important qualities--the quality of our telecommunications link, and the quality of the product at the end of that link. Various branches of government are currently putting most of the product at the end of the link. Companies will follow.

CONSEQUENCES FOR DISTRICT PLANNING

The nice thing about the future is that everyone can predict it, and if you are wrong, who's going to remember? The problem for teachers is that the future is not some distant activity, it is decisions you have to make now. No one wants another room full of Commodore 64s or an AV lab filled with Beta tape players. Our resources are limited. Besides no one likes looking stupid.

So, how can we improve our odds of being on the VHS/Macintosh side of the technology divide? There are at least a few directions that seem relatively certain.

1. Optical fiber is replacing twisted pair. In general, schools are over-building, putting in as much wiring capacity as they can on the assumption that we will be moving from text transfer to video transfer, and that will require the bandwidth of fiber. Copper may be enough for short hops, but fiber is needed for main sections of the district WAN. We will be pushing more data down the WAN, not less, so we need to plan for more capacity than may currently be needed. This seems wise.

2. Network activities are overwhelming all other activities. UW-Stevens Point has two computer labs that aren't connected to email. They are fine for word processing or most other academic activities. Students won't use them. They will stand in line to get to the nine other labs that are on the Net. It won't be enough for schools to wire up one lab and say that is the email lab, and use the other labs for other kinds of software. Those other labs will become relics collecting dust and teachers teaching touch typing. Internet connectivity will have to be brought to all the computers in the school.

3. Internet costs will go up, not down. Sincere efforts are being made by telephone companies to bring down phone charges for schools. But remember Rothstein's figures that telephone charges are just 11% of total connectivity costs. As we bring more teachers and more students onto the Net, our costs for teacher training and computer support will mushroom. Any district administrator who doesn't budget accordingly is headed for a very unpleasant surprise. A planning committee I was on for the University of Wisconsin System once calculated that IBM could bankrupt the university by donating ten thousand computers to us. We could never cover the support costs. Free long distance time has the same potential.

4. The reasons for getting on the Net will become nearly irresistible. Now the Internet is a curiosity, a business tool, and an educational extra. You get patted on the back if you are on-line, but no one looks too oddly at you if you haven't connected yet. That is changing. Committees of the National Council of Teachers of English meet on-line. Their resources are shared on-line. To be *off*-line is to be cut off from one's professional colleagues. Meanwhile, the millions of computers sold for home use (the number one

Christmas present in both 1994 and 1995) had two features in common--a CD-ROM drive and a modem. Our sense of fair play will drive us to try to give all our students access to resources many of our students have at home.

5. The Internet will be packaged as neatly as a textbook series. Our online pioneers are happy to explore for resources and figure out how to make the hardware work and how to teach it and test it. These are the same people who found value in microcomputers back when computers couldn't do much more than run your programs in BASIC. Then the settlers arrived and worked the labs with the help of packages supplied by Scholastic and the Learning Company. On-line packages are being shrink-wrapped as we speak. The prairie will be fenced in and average folks will raise crops there. It will all become pretty and painless. Meanwhile, the pioneers can still "light out for the territories."

 # DISCUSSION QUESTIONS

1. What do you think the on-line resources in your school will look like in five years? What forces make you optimistic? Which make you pessimistic?

2. What prediction errors are you most concerned about? Which would cost your district the most money?

3. What general technology trends are you hearing about that might impact this area?

4. What companies do you think will become players in this area?

5. What do you think teacher training in this area will look like in five years?

Appendix
Web Sites for Schools

This book and the PBS course have a Web site with links to educational materials. The address of the Web site is:

http://www.uwsp.edu/acad/math/infohwy.html

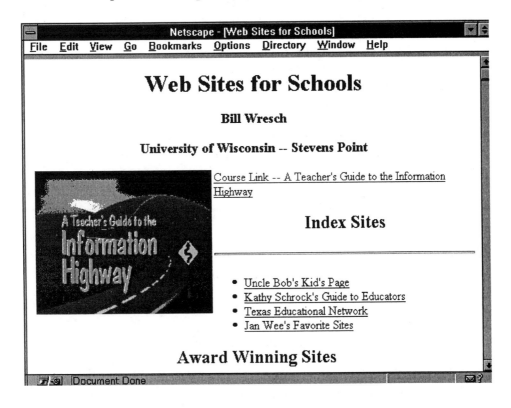

This site will provide you with a wide range of current resources. Below is a partial list of the Web links available from this site. No complete list of Web sites for schools is possible--there are just too many. But these sites should get you started.

 Warning: Sites move. Addresses change. Not every site listed here will be exactly in the address shown.

Index Sites

Start with these first--each will lead you to many more sites in every subject area.

- **Uncle Bob's Kid's Page**
  http://gagme.wwa.com/~boba/kids.html

- **Kathy Schrock's Guide to Educators**
  http://www.capecod.net/Wixon/wixon.htm

- **Texas Educational Network**
  http://www.tenet.edu

- **Jan Wee's Favorite Sites**
  http://www.state.wi.us/agencies/dpi/www/jan_fav.html

Award Winning Sites

These sites were given an A+ rating in 1996 by *Classroom Connect*

- **ERIC** (Educational Resources Information Center)
  http://ericir.syr.edu

- **Developing Educational Standards**
  http://putwest.boces.org/Standards.html

- **Cells Alive**
  http://www.comet.net/quill

- **Eisenhower National Clearinghouse**
  http://www.enc.org

- **Pet Pages**
  http://www.dynamo.net/dynamo/pets/pets.html

- **ArtsEdNet**
  http://www.artsednet.getty.edu

- **Armadillo**
  http://chico.rice.edu/armadillo

- **Volcano World**
  http://volcano.und.nodak.edu

- **Nine Planets Tour**
  http://seds.lpl.arizona.edu/nineplanets/nineplanets/nineplanets.html

- **Pathways to School Improvement**
  http://www.ncrel.org/ncrel/sdrs/pathways.htm

- **Froggy Page**
  http://www.cs.yale.edu/homes/sjl/froggy.html

- **MegaMath**
  http://www.c3.lanl.gov:80/mega-math/

- **Children's Literature Web Guide**
  http://www.ucalgary.ca/~dkbrown/index.html

- **Virtual Tourist II**
  http://www.vtourist.com/vt/

- **Janice's K12 Outpost**
  http://k12.cnidr.org/janice_k12/k12menu.html

- **Reasons for the Internet in K12 Schools**
  http://www.sils.umich.edu/Community/Students/kenh/k12.html

- **Web66**
  http://web66.coled.umn.edu

- **Academy One**
  http://www.nptn.org/cyber.serv/AOneP/

- **Complete Works of Shakespeare**
  http://the-tech.mit.edu/Shakespeare

- **From Now On: A Monthly Commentary on Educational Technology Issues**
  http://www.pacificrim.net/~mckenzie/

- **Global SchoolNet**
  http://gsn.org

- **KidsCom**
  http://www.spectracom.com

- **Exploratorium**
  http://www.exploratorium.edu

- **Carlos' Interactive Coloring Book**
  http://www.ravenna.com/coloring/

- **Uncle Bob's Kids Page**
  http://gagme.wwa.com/~boba/kids.html

- **WebLouvre**
  http://mistral.enst.fr/~pioch/louvre/

- **Global Show & Tell Online**
  http://emma.manymedia.com:80/show-n-tell/

- **Intercultural E-Mail Classroom Connections (IECC)**
  http://www.stolaf.edu/network/iecc/

Arts

- **Getty Center for Education in the Arts**
  http://www.artsednet.getty.edu

- **Web Louvre**
  http://sunsite.unc.edu/louvre

Astronomy

- **Comets**
  http://www.comet.arc.nasa.gov/comet

- **NASA**
  http://www.nasa.gov

- **Project Galileo**
  http://www.jpl.nasa.gov:80/galileo

- **Shuttle Flights**
  http://www.osf.hq.nasa.gov/flights.html

- **Space Station**
  http://www.osf.hq.nasa.gov/iss

Biology

- **Access Excellence**
  http://www.gene.com/ae/

- **Biotechnology--Genentech**
  http://cns.bio.com:80/resedu/educate.html

- **Biotechnology--University of Wisconsin**
  http://www.biotech.wisc.edu

- **Cells Alive**
  http://www.comet.chv.va.us/quill

- **Dinosaurs--Chicago Field Museum**
  http://www.bvis.uic.edu/museum/exhibits

- **Dinosaurs--UC Berkeley**
  http://ucmp1.berkeley.edu/exhibittext/dinosaur.html

- **Dinosaur fossils**
  http://www.hcc.hawaii.edu/dinos/

- **Dinosaur excavation site**
  http://freenet.calgary.ab.ca/science/tyrrell

- **Frog Dissection**
  http://george.lbl.gov/vfrog

- **Magic School Bus**
  http://www.scholastic.com

- **Project Jason**
  http://seawifs.gsfc.nasa.gov/jason.html

- **Seaworld**
  http://www.bev.net/education/SeaWorld/homepage.html

Chemistry

- **ACS Division of Chemical Education**
  http://www.acs.org/edugen2/education/aboutedu.htm

- **Beakman's World**
  http://www.spe.sony.com/Pictures/tv/beakman/facts.html

- **Bill Nye the Science Guy**
  http://nyelabds.kcts.org

- **National Science Education Standards**
  http://www.nap.edu/nap/online/nses/html/overview.html#teaching

- **National Science Foundation**
  http://www.nsf.gov

- **National Science Teachers Association**
  http://www.nsta.org

- **Newton's Apple Teacher Guides**
  http://www.mnonline.org/ktca/newtons/alpha.html

- **NPR Science Friday Kids Connection**
  http://www.npr.org/sfkids/

Current Events

- **Campaign 96**
  http://campaign.96.com

- **Chicago Tribune**
  http://www.chicago.tribune.com

- **CNN**
  http://www.cnn.com

- **Current Events**
  http://www.yahoo.com/News/Current_events

- **Fed World**
  http://www.fedworld.gov

- **New York Times**
  http://www.nytimes.com

- **Thomas**
  http://thomas.loc.gov

- **The White House**
  http://www.Whitehouse.gov/WH/Welcome.html

Education

- **ERIC**
  http://ericir.syr.edu

- **Lesson Plans**
  http://www.teachnet.com

- **School Improvement Planning**
  http://www.ncrel.org/ncrel/sdrs/pathways.htm

- **US Dept of Education**
  http://www.ed.gov

English

- **Children's Literature**
  http://www.ucalgary.ca/~dkbrown/index.html

- **Inkspot**
  http://www.interlog.com/~ohi/inkspot/

- **Kids Pub**
  http://www.en-grade.com/kidpub/

- **Mythology**
  http://www.computek.net/public/barr/classic.html

- **National Council of Techers of English**
  http://www.ncte.org

- **Purdue On-Line Writing Lab**
  http://owl.trc.purdue.edu/prose.html

- **Shakespeare**
  http://the-tech.mit.edu/Shakespeare

- **Word Web**
  http://syndicate.com/nectar.html

- **Writer's Resources**
  http://www.interlog.com~chi/www/writesource.html

- **Writing**
  http://www.computek.net/public/barr/creativewriting.html

Foreign Languages

- **ABC Newspaper (Spanish)**
  http://www.abc.es

- **International Cultural Exchange**
  http://www.stolaf.edu/network/iecc

- **Kids Window on Japan**
  http://jw.stanford.edu

- **Spanish Culture**
  http://www.DocuWeb.ca/SiSpain/sp-home.html

Foreign Schools

Use these links to make contact with schools around the world.

- **Directory of South African Schools**
  http://www.icon.co.za/~matthew/schoolza.html

- **Western Cape Schools (South Africa)**
  http://www.wcape.school.za

- **Eastern Cape Schools (South Africa)**
  http://www.ecape.school.za

- **University of Cape Town**
  http://www.uct.ac.za

- **Intercultural E-Mail Classroom Connections (IECC)**
  http://www.stolaf.edu/network/iecc/

- **Web66 International Schools Registry**
  http://web66.coled.umn.edu

Geography/Geology

- **Earthquakes**
  http://quake.wr.usgs.gov

- **Mapquest**
  http://www.mapquest.com

- **US Geological Survey**
  http://www.usgs.gov

- **Virtual Tourist**
  http://www.vtourist.com/vt

- **Volcanoes**
  http://volcano.und.nodak.edu

- **Weather**
  http://www.nnic.noaa.gov/cgi-bin/page?pg=netcast

History

- **Civil War**
  http://funnelweb.utcc.utk.edu/~hoemann/cwarhp.html

- **US Holocaust Museum**
  http://www.ushmn.org

- **Virtual Library--History**
  http://kuhttp.cc.ukans.edu/history/WWW_history_main.html

Internet Issues

- **Alta Vista--Search Engine**
  http://www.altavista.digital.com

- **Classroom Connect**
  http://www.classroom.net
- **The Silence Project**
  http://www.uwsp.edu/acad/math/silence.html

- **WebCrawler--Search Engine**
  http://webcrawler.com

- **Yahoo--Search Engine**
  http://www.yahoo.com

Math

- **Dave's Math Tables**
  http://www.sisweb.com/math/tables.html

- **Eric's Treasure Trove Project**
  http://www.gps.caltech.edu/~eww/math/math0.html

- **History of Math**
  http://www-groups.dcs.st-and.ac.uk:80/~history

- **Math Archive**
  http://archives.math.utk.edu

- **Mathematics Careers**
  http://www.ams.org/careers/mcbb.html

- **Math Forum** (*also* **Ask Dr. Math** *and* **Math Magic**)
  http://forum.swarthmore.edu

- **Mathematical Association of America**
  http://math.maa.org

- **MegaMath**
  http://www.c3.lanl.gov:80/mega-math/

- **National Council of Teachers of Mathematics**
  http://www.nctm.org

- **Statistical Lesson Plans**
  http://www.ncsa.uiuc.edu:80/Edu/MSTE/meseke/plans.html
- **Teacher's Page of Mathematics**
  http://www.ualberta.ca/~bleeck/math.html

Web Page Creation

- **Web Index--Listing of HTML Resources**
  http://www.utirc.utoronto.ca/htmldocs/NewHTML/htmlindex.html

- **HTML Tools**
  http://www.utirc.utoronto.ca/htmldocs/misc_tools.html

- **An Online Book on HTML**
  http://shu.edu/docs/about/html/html_bas.html